SAVING MY SISTER

SAVING MY SISTER

HOW I CREATED MEANING
from ADDICTION *and* LOSS

NICOLE DAVIS WOODRUFF

LIONCREST
PUBLISHING

Hardcover ISBN: 978-1-5445-2952-3
Paperback ISBN: 978-1-5445-2951-6
Ebook ISBN: 978-1-5445-2950-9

Note to the reader

Because of the complexity of the numerous dates surrounding the events in Amanda's story, I have included a timeline of events as an appendix at the end of the book for clarity.

Content warning:

Although this book was written to shed light on many of these issues, it should be known that stories of drug use, accidental overdose, and death can be difficult for many readers. Discretion is advised.

To my sister Amanda, I love and miss you every day...

CONTENTS

INTRODUCTION
xiii

CHAPTER 1
THE FIRST TIME
1

CHAPTER 2
PARTNER IN CRIME
11

CHAPTER 3
THE MAKING OF A MONSTER
23

CHAPTER 4
2016: THE YEAR THAT CHANGED EVERYTHING
37

CHAPTER 5
THE AFTERMATH
51

CHAPTER 6

ENOUGH IS ENOUGH
63

CHAPTER 7

FINALLY, A NEW ROCK BOTTOM
73

CHAPTER 8

TOUGH LOVE
85

CHAPTER 9

LONGEST STRETCH OF SOBRIETY
93

CHAPTER 10

A NEW APPROACH TO RELAPSE
105

CHAPTER 11

HISTORY REPEATING
113

CHAPTER 12

HISTORY NOT REPEATING
125

CHAPTER 13

SHE HAS TO SAVE HERSELF
133

CHAPTER 14

WHERE IS SHE?
143

CHAPTER 15

THERE'S NO WAKING UP FROM THIS NIGHTMARE
155

CHAPTER 16

SEARCHING FOR ANSWERS
165

CHAPTER 17

IN MEMORIAM
175

CHAPTER 18

LESSONS
181

ACKNOWLEDGMENTS
191

APPENDIX:
TIMELINE OF EVENTS
193

INTRODUCTION

I could tell by the sound of my mom's voice that it was probably a good idea to pull over.

"Nicole?!" she said anxiously.

"What happened, Mom?"

Her pain cut through me as she stumbled over her words on the phone. "I just found your sister and Mitch on the floor. They must've done heroin and passed out. I struggled waking them up. Amanda didn't know what time it was or remember that Christopher needed to be picked up from school. I'm going to pick him up now and take him to my house."

I took the next exit on I-65 and pulled over at the closest gas station.

"Okay, Mom. I'll call you right back. I need to call my patient and tell him I'll be late."

Moments before the call, I had been peacefully driving down I-65 to my next patient. It was April 2016. Spring had finally sprung in Nashville, Tennessee, and I was taking in the scenery of the blooming dogwoods with my window down just slightly to feel the spring breeze against my cheek. As a home health occupational therapist, I drove all over Nashville to provide therapy to patients within their homes. I wouldn't say I loved everything about my job, but I certainly enjoyed the flexibility and the breaks I had driving between patients. It was a time to unwind and listen to my favorite podcasts, all while being paid to travel. A definite perk in my book.

Most days were pretty uneventful, but today wasn't like most days. Today had been a *good day*. I wasn't ready to let go of that just yet. But I didn't have a choice. Before I even answered the phone, I felt the heaviness in my chest. I knew it had to be about my sister, Amanda. It always was.

I called my patient and tried my best to hold it together while I explained I would be late. After taking a moment to breathe, I called my mom back. I was happy I'd pulled over because the emotion that came over me was uncontrollable. I closed my eyes and let the rage sink in as I listened to the ringing through the phone. Once again, my sister had used heroin and my mom was left to pick up the pieces of Amanda's messy life. I hated that my mom had to deal with this stuff on her own; I always wanted to protect her.

"Hello?" she answered solemnly.

"Hey. I'm so sorry you have to deal with this today. What can I do to help?"

"I just took Christopher back to my house. He's doing okay. Doesn't seem too worried about Amanda right now; he's playing in the living room. Maybe you can call and talk to her. I don't know what else to do at this point."

"Okay, I'll try calling her. I don't know what to say either, though, Mom. She obviously needs help but won't admit it."

"I've had enough, Nicole. I'm going to have a heart attack over this. I literally cannot handle it."

"Okay, I'll see what I can do. I'll call you back."

I hung up the phone. I let out a huge scream and prepared to call my sister. I couldn't believe we were dealing with this shit *yet again!* What was I going to say to Amanda? Would she even answer the phone? Why was I the one who always had to manage her shit? She wasn't going to tell me the truth anyway. This whole thing was exhausting.

This wasn't the first time, and most certainly would not be the last time my sister would use heroin. It was a long, drawn-out journey dating back to her college days. That was when she started taking opioids.

In January 2014, my sister tried heroin for the first time. From that moment on, our lives would never be the same. I have said for years that injecting heroin into your body is like selling your soul to the devil. The addiction that follows is all-consuming, unwavering, and intoxicatingly manipulating. It destroys individuals, families, relationships, careers, lives. You name it—if you cared about it before heroin, you may as well consider it gone after you inject that very first dose. At least that's my experience, watching my sister transform into a person I could not recognize after years of heroin addiction.

Thankfully, I don't know this type of addiction firsthand. But what I do know is addiction is not an individual disease. It's a family disease. I'll never be able to erase the memories of watching my parents suffer and worry every day because of my sister. I'll never forget how my sister slurred her words and nodded off while sitting in my mother's living room, yet denied she was even on drugs. And I'll never unsee how each member of my family grieved—and is still struggling today—as a result of her addiction.

Having a substance use disorder and loving someone with this disease are two very different sides of the same coin of addiction. Amanda and I had planned on someday using this book to share how these stories look very different from the perspective of the person with addiction versus the perspective of a family member or loved one. During her longest stretch of sobriety, in 2018, we discussed what this would look like and how we could make it happen. We were talking on the phone one day and I said, "You know what? We should write a book about your story and how your journey to sobriety looked so much different from your perspective versus mine. I really think we could make a big impact with a book like that." She laughed and said, "Hell, if you'll write it, I'm down. Let's do it!"

From that moment on, we talked almost weekly about writing a book together. We bounced ideas off each other and brainstormed how we could intertwine our stories. However, at the time, I was working nonstop, and Amanda was busy adjusting to life in early recovery, so it always felt more like a "someday thing" for both of us.

Unfortunately, that "someday" never happened.

On June 13, 2019, just over five years after she first tried heroin, Amanda passed away from an opioid overdose. After she died, I knew with every fiber of my being that I needed to write this book. I needed to do it for her. And for me. And for everyone else who is impacted in one way or another by the horrible disease of addiction. So, although Amanda did not survive her addiction and was not able to share her side in this book, I like to believe she was with me every step of the way while I wrote and helped me recall details of the events that happened, even if only from my perspective.

This is our story. The story of my sister Amanda, the progression of her addiction, and the consequences of her decisions along the way. And this is my story. The story of my grief, hope, frustration, disappointment, and everything in between. Whether you have personally experienced opioid addiction, or you are a family member or loved one of someone with this disease, I hope reading this will impact you in some way or another. There are millions of us going through this shit every single day. It's time we share our stories.

CHAPTER 1

THE FIRST TIME

The first time my sister overdosed on heroin was in January 2014. I'll never forget that day for the rest of my life. I was still living at home with my mom and stepdad, working at my first job in a skilled nursing facility after graduating college with my occupational therapy degree. I remember being at work and seeing that my mom was calling me, which I knew was never a good sign, as she would usually text or wait to tell me something when I got home. I answered, worried what she might say.

"Nicole?" She sounded panicked.

"Yes," I answered.

"Your sister just called me and told me she is stuck in Allentown at the hospital. She was with *that guy*, Joe. She said he injected her with heroin and left her to die."

"*What?* Are you sure? You've got to be kidding me." I fumbled over my words, lost in disbelief.

"Yes, she just called me. She needs someone to go down there and get her. Joe took off with her car and everything. I don't know what to do because I'm working."

SOS. Total panic came over me. It felt like my heart fell into my chest and I lost the ability to breathe. Even after all the years of dealing with Amanda shadily taking pills, I was still unprepared to hear my mom say these words.

This was literally our worst nightmare. Amanda was my only sibling, and this news rattled me to my core. She always swore that she would never touch heroin. I remember her specifically telling me, a few years prior to this overdose, "You know I would be in a really bad place if I were ever to use heroin. That stuff is *nasty*. I'll never fuck with that."

I mean, I guess I should have expected this day to come. Amanda had been on and off prescription opiates for years, with a long history of abuse, since before her son, Christopher, was born in 2008. After multiple car accidents in her early twenties, she developed chronic pain and was diagnosed with fibromyalgia. Amanda never found alternative therapies to manage her pain and relied on narcotic pain medications. She started with tramadol, then moved onto Vicodin, then Percocet…you get the picture.

After Christopher was born, she went into a depression and leaned on opiates to make herself feel better. A few months into this cycle, she admitted to having an opiate addiction and taking around twenty Vicodin pills per day. This was the first time she had ever outwardly admitted to having a problem with substance abuse. She told my family, her doctor, and Christopher's father, who was still her boyfriend at the time. She had some tough discussions with my parents and Christopher's father, and they all supported her in getting the treatment she needed. She started outpatient drug counseling and committed to getting better for herself and her son.

I remember feeling confused back then because I didn't understand substance use disorders. I knew taking twenty pills a day was an awful lot, but I thought that with counseling, she would overcome it. However, I was only nineteen years old at the time and didn't understand the challenges of new mother-hood, postpartum depression, and the struggles Amanda was facing as a young mom. She was only twenty-three when she was thrust into motherhood as the result of an accidental preg-nancy. She and Christopher's father had only been dating for a few months when they found out she was pregnant. She was still getting to know him as she navigated pregnancy, moving back home to live closer to family, and the hardships of early motherhood.

As the mom of a young toddler myself, I now know those hardships *oh so well* but did not understand at all in 2008. Looking back, I can see how a predisposition to addiction can spiral out of control when you add in postpartum depression. I wish my family and I had a better understanding of what Amanda was going through. She didn't breastfeed, but she was still feeding a baby around the clock. Add in lack of sleep, body changes, hormonal shifts, and discovering her identity as a mom—it was a whole new world for her. I didn't understand these things at all. I wish I could say my parents did, but after having my first child last year, I quickly learned they do *not* remember what it is like to raise a newborn.

Maybe if we all had understood what Amanda was going through at the time, we could have offered her more support to prevent her disease from progressing. Unfortunately, we were uneducated and ignorant to the challenges she was facing as a young mother dealing with substance use disorder. So here we were, five years later, trying to clean up the mess of her first heroin overdose.

I felt angry, disappointed, frustrated, and confused. So many emotions all at the same time. I didn't know what to say to my mom, but I knew she couldn't handle this on her own. My mom is fragile and doesn't handle stress well. I knew I would have to step up and take care of this situation. I just didn't understand how we had gotten here. How did Amanda go from taking prescription pills to overdosing on heroin?

I decided to turn these thoughts off for the time being and went into what I call "handle it" mode. My shock still in overdrive, I told my boss I needed to leave early and briefly explained the situation as I ran out of the therapy gym and nursing facility where I worked. My mom picked up Christopher from school, and after I left work, I drove more than an hour to get Amanda from the emergency department of the Lehigh Valley Hospital.

As I drove to the hospital, I felt anxious and didn't know what to expect. I had never seen anyone on heroin before. I could only picture what I had seen in the media: someone slumped over on the side of the street after sticking a needle in their arm. What would Amanda look like? Would she even be able to talk to me? I was about to find out.

I pulled in front of the hospital and waited for her to come outside. After a few minutes, Amanda approached my vehicle and flashed what looked like a drunken smile. She flung herself into my car and said hello. Her eyes were barely open, and she looked exhausted.

At first, I just drove, staring at the road ahead as my shock wore off. What was the best way to approach this? I wanted answers, but she wasn't in the right state of mind to give them. After a while, I finally asked, "So why did you do it? I thought you said you'd never do heroin." She mumbled, "I dunno…I just wanted to."

Her breathing was loud and heavy. Out of the corner of my eye, I could see her thick brown hair whipping back and forth as she swayed in my passenger seat. We spoke sparingly, mostly just me asking questions and her responding with short, one-word answers. Her speech was slurred, and I could tell it was difficult for her to even process what I was saying. Eventually, I just let it go. She wasn't in the right state of mind to talk, so I decided it would be best to wait until the morning. For the rest of the trip, she was either nodding off or asleep. She had no clue what was going on; she just knew that she was with me and I was taking her home. She was safe, for now.

I'll never forget that drive for the rest of my life. I couldn't believe what Amanda looked like, how she spoke to me, or the effects heroin still had on her, even hours after she had used. And *long* after Narcan had been administered. Narcan is an opioid antagonist that immediately begins to reverse the effects of an opioid overdose. At the time, in 2014, I was not well-versed in opioid addiction, and because this was Amanda's first overdose, I had never heard of Narcan. Now I know all about it, as it saved my sister's life more times than I can count. This was just the first.

When we got home, I decided to stay the night at her place so I could keep an eye on her. I didn't trust her to be alone. I wanted to make sure she was okay and wouldn't use any more heroin for the rest of the night. I planned to call out of work in the morning so I could arrange for her to go to rehab and get the help she needed. In her stupor, she had agreed to go to rehab, so I was hopeful we could find a place for her to go the very next day. Christopher was staying at my mom's and, thankfully, did not have to witness what I'd just seen over the last few hours.

The next morning when we woke up, Amanda was not feeling well. She was tired and complained of being in a lot of pain, which was nothing new for her. She had fibromyalgia, so this was an everyday complaint. With the added effects of heroin withdrawal, I imagine that pain was a bit more intense. So, while she lay around on the couch, I started making phone calls to find her a rehab facility. I called numerous facilities and struggled to find quality programs that accepted her Medicaid insurance.

My friend's brother had gone to a privately owned rehab facility in Pennsylvania about a year prior. He'd had a positive experience and was still in recovery. The facility was known for expert addiction recovery specialists, supportive programs, and connections to elite transitional programs after discharge. I had heard there were possible scholarships available, so this facility was the first place I called. I thought, *Wow, if I could just get her in* here, *she would have exactly what she needs to get better.*

Unfortunately, they did not have a scholarship available to offer Amanda. And I quickly learned the cost of these private facilities is *very* high. The admissions coordinator explained that it would cost several thousand dollars just to reserve her spot. She said, "Many families liquidate 401(k)s or refinance their homes in order to pay for treatment." This sounded absurd to me. Who could afford this type of care? And if you do pay for it, who says that treatment will actually work? Sadly, my family couldn't afford to pay for Amanda to go to a privately owned facility. I hung up the phone, disappointed and desperate to find her help.

After several hours of research, I found some facilities funded by the state that accepted Amanda's Medicaid insurance. A few calls later, I learned she needed to have a drug and alcohol assessment performed by the county; from there, they would recommend treatment options. I was hopeful they would recommend an inpatient program, as I feared she would not get what she needed from outpatient treatment. In her grogginess, she agreed to let me take her for the evaluation. I scheduled her for an appointment later that afternoon.

As I drove Amanda to her appointment, I couldn't help but see the lack of drive in her face. She just sat in the passenger seat and stared ahead, expressionless. It seemed like she didn't really care at all and was just coming along to please me. I hated seeing her act that way, but I was also proud of her for agreeing to go to the appointment in the first place.

When we got there, staff greeted us both in the waiting area and asked Amanda to fill out some forms. After a few minutes, a counselor came out and called Amanda's name. I stood up to go with her, but the counselor wouldn't let me go back for the assessment. This worried me: I feared she wouldn't tell them the whole story, the truth about what had happened, or the severity of her issues over the years. This may have been the first time she used heroin, but it was definitely not the start of her drug use. I whispered to Amanda, "Be honest," and sat back down to wait for her.

After forty-five minutes, Amanda reappeared in the waiting area and told me she would be going to an inpatient facility about an hour from home. The facility had a bed open, and she would be going the next day.

I let out a sigh of relief. I was thrilled and thought this could be the solution to getting her the help she so desperately needed. I was willing to do whatever it took to get her there, including paying for all the items she requested to take with her: toiletries, makeup, a carton of cigarettes, and spending money. This was Amanda's first time going to rehab, and I was hopeful it would be her last. Of course, I worried it wouldn't be that easy, but she had never gone to rehab before. I thought this overdose would be a wake-up call for her and that it might have scared her enough to stay away from heroin. I hoped that, with proper treatment, she would recognize the severity of her decision to use drugs and find better coping skills to handle stress and manage her cravings for opiates. I recognize now that a "one and done" stint in rehab is unlikely, but back then, I was naively optimistic.

The following day, after getting everything she needed, I drove her to the rehab facility, where she would stay for the next twenty-eight days. She didn't say much on the way there but seemed eager to get help and get back home to her son. She knew she had really messed up and didn't want him to know the severity of what had happened. He would be staying at my mom's while she went into treatment. My mom, my stepdad, and I would take care of him and make sure he got everything he needed while Amanda was away. Without knowing what else to say, we told him that his mommy was sick and needed to go away for a little while to get better, but we promised Christopher she was okay and would be back soon. His dad was not very involved at this point, so his mom was all he knew.

When we arrived at the treatment facility, I was surprised by how secluded it was. We had never been to this town before, but it wasn't much different from where we lived—the middle of nowhere, Pennsylvania. Seeing it gave me the confidence that if she tried to leave, there wasn't anywhere for her to go.

We sat in the intake area for a while, waiting for her to be admitted. We learned that she had brought some things that I needed to take home because they were not permitted. I had never really thought about what you're allowed to take to rehab—but you learn new things every day. Apparently, aerosol hairsprays and mouthwash were a no go. Luckily, everything else she'd brought was allowed, and Amanda could survive without hairspray for the next month.

After intake was complete, that was the end of the road for me. I was not allowed to go back with her to her room, so we said our goodbyes. I told her to take things seriously and to make sure she wrote to me at least once or twice and called to keep me updated. She agreed, and with her smug smile, she said, "I love you, Nicole. Don't worry; I'll be fine." I drove home that night and hoped for the best—it was all I could do.

CHAPTER 2

PARTNER IN CRIME

While Amanda was in rehab from January to February 2014, she wrote me a letter that made me feel optimistic about her experience. She thanked me for finding her a place to go and for being there for her during such a difficult time. She wrote about everything she was learning and apologized for disappointing our family. She even said, "There are people here who have been to rehab 5–10+ times and that is NOT going to be me. I can't wait to come home to my baby."

I felt hopeful about her return home. I was proud of her, and honestly, it felt like things couldn't have gone much better. After her overdose, she called my mom and owned up to what happened. She admitted to having a problem and was agreeable to treatment. And we got her into rehab immediately. As far as best-case scenarios go, it felt like we had hit a home run.

Amanda stayed in rehab for twenty-eight days, which is the typical length of stay for acute inpatient rehab. Since this was her first time, we weren't too familiar with aftercare, recovery, or halfway houses. I wish we had known more. Amanda told us she would be going to outpatient drug counseling, which was set up for her by the facility prior to her discharge. We believed her when she said she was done using heroin, and we trusted that she would continue her journey in recovery through outpatient counseling. Unfortunately, we were naive.

Looking back now, I should have pushed harder for her to go to a recovery house after rehab. I didn't understand how important that transition out of treatment is for long-term success in sobriety. I've since learned that the initial twenty-eight days of treatment is only the beginning, and what happens immediately after discharge—having the appropriate support system and environment—is absolutely *crucial* to long-term recovery. I also wasn't prepared for the types of relationships people with addiction can form with each other while in treatment. Amanda quickly proved to me that *going to rehab versus being committed to recovery* are two entirely different things. And the people you meet in treatment along the way can highly influence that journey in early recovery. Unfortunately, Amanda formed a close friendship with someone who had been in and out of rehab many times. She met her new "partner in crime."

Amanda came home from rehab on a Tuesday. The facility provided her with transportation, so I didn't have to worry about driving to pick her up. Christopher could not stop talking about how excited he was to finally see her, so my mom dropped him off at Amanda's apartment after school. Unfortunately, my mom had to work in the evening, so she couldn't stay with him the entire time. After I finished work, I stopped by Amanda's place to check in and visit for a while. I approached the door and smiled. I was about to have my first conversation in years with my *sober* sister. I felt so grateful and excited to see her.

As I walked inside, I saw six-year-old Christopher sitting in the living room by himself, playing with his toys. I greeted him with a hug, and he jumped up in excitement to see me. I asked where his mommy was, and he pointed me toward the kitchen. As I walked through the living room and into the kitchen, I smelled cigarette smoke and heard the sound of two voices talking. I was confused—Amanda hadn't mentioned having company when I'd talked to her earlier.

My eyes burned a little when I walked into the smoky kitchen. Amanda sat at the table, puffing on a cigarette, dressed in a baggy T-shirt with her hair pulled back, not a care in the world. Across from her was a girl, probably about my age or a year or two older, with short brown hair and glazed-over eyes. Concern and confusion were written across my face. Amanda casually greeted me. "Hey, Nicole. This is Shannon."

I froze. "Uh…Hi, Shannon. How do you two know each other?"

Amanda explained that they had met in rehab and Shannon had come over to "hang out for a few days." I nodded my head in understanding, carefully considering what to say next.

"Why aren't you spending time with Christopher?" I asked.

"I was. He's in there playing. Why, what's wrong?"

"Nothing's wrong. I'm just a little concerned as to why you're in here smoking and not paying attention to him after being gone for almost a month."

"Oh, here we go already. Nicole, he's fine. I'm not in the mood for this shit," Amanda spat back at me.

And there it was—Amanda already getting defensive. Looking back, I most definitely should not have confronted her this way, but I was in complete shock. I had expected an entirely different situation prior to stepping inside her apartment. I thought I would find my now *sober* sister interacting with her son and enjoying their time together. Unfortunately, that's not what I walked into, and I let my emotions and shock get the best of me.

Knowing what I know now, I would have approached the situation much differently and would not have been so harsh, asking Amanda those tough questions right off the bat. This is important because the moment anyone had any suspicions about her behavior or confronted her, Amanda became defensive and upset, which always led to a fight. Years later, in 2021, I recognize this and would have reacted differently, at least on the outside. But I was twenty-four years old and had never dealt with this situation before. Immediately asking Amanda these accusatory questions was an emotional reaction that I would not recommend others do in this situation. Instead, I would recommend breathing, observing, and trying not to get emotional or upset. Trust me—I understand this is difficult. But as you'll see later, a calmer approach always works better when communicating with someone who is actively using.

Getting back to Amanda's first night out of rehab, I finally realized I wasn't going to get anywhere by asking Amanda questions she didn't want to answer. I took a deep breath and contemplated how I was going to handle the situation. Amanda was completely uninterested in her son and couldn't have cared less that he was playing by himself in the living room. She scrolled through her cell phone and continued to puff on her cigarette. As I stood there in shock, I noticed Shannon seemed a bit *off*.

From across the room, I watched as Shannon repeatedly nodded off and slurred her words every time she attempted to speak. Sporadically, she would come out of it and say, "Sorry, it must be my Seroquel making me so sleepy." I was skeptical and didn't know exactly what I was witnessing, but these two did not seem "rehabilitated," to say the least.

My heart was breaking. I had so much hope and had envisioned an entirely different scenario when I walked into Amanda's apartment. The disappointment washed over me as I watched them. It was obvious they were both under the influence of some type of drug, most likely heroin, judging by how tired they looked. I can still feel my frustration as I stood there watching them. This was when I knew that drug rehab programs only work if the person is ready to change. And it was pretty darn obvious no one in that kitchen was in any hurry to change.

I asked Amanda if they had been using, but of course, she quickly denied being on any drugs. As Shannon continued to nod off and Amanda fumbled with her phone and lit another cigarette, I decided I couldn't take much more. I walked back out to the living room and told Christopher to get ready because we would be going back to Grammy's house. I helped him clean up his toys and put his coat on. I took a deep breath before going back into the kitchen.

"Amanda, we're leaving. I'm going to take Christopher with me. We'll keep him at Mom's house until you get yourself settled."

I wanted her to agree with this, so I chose my words wisely to not upset her. I held my breath as she turned to us and quickly agreed. "Okay, that's fine. Come say bye to

Mommy, baby." Christopher approached the table where she sat. Amanda wrapped an arm around him and said goodbye.

Well, that was easier than I thought. At least she didn't argue with me. I told Amanda I would call her in the morning, even though that was the last thing I felt like doing.

To say I was disappointed would be an understatement. I could not understand how a mother could be away from her son for almost a month and then come home and act this way. Did she even miss him at all? Did she take him for granted? It was disheartening.

We planned for Christopher to stay with us at my mom's house for a while, at least until Amanda decided to act like a mother again. It was hard, though—how do you explain this to a six year old? "Sorry, your mommy is on drugs and is too concerned about her new friend to pay attention to you." Of course not. We couldn't say anything close to the truth. So we lied, and we tried to make the best of the situation so he was taken care of. That was all we could do.

We told him, "Your mommy is still getting better. You'll see her soon, though. We promise." "Don't worry. Mommy will be visiting soon." We distracted him the best we could. We took him to places like Chuck E. Cheese and movie theaters. We entertained him at home with games and lots of playtime. We worked on homework and made sure he was doing everything he needed to do for school. We played outside in the snow. We kept him busy. It was all we could do.

As the rest of this week went on, we didn't hear much from Amanda. My frustration grew every day as she continued to pretend she didn't have a six-year-old son living just a few minutes away at my mom's house. I didn't fully understand what was going on until a few days later, on Saturday morning, when we got an unexpected phone call.

My mom answered the phone. It was Amanda calling from a hospital. I could hear my mom arguing with Amanda as she tried to understand what was going on. She hated dealing with these situations, especially when Amanda became argumentative and wouldn't tell the whole story. Remember what I said about too many tough questions leading to a fight? That sums up every interaction my mom had with Amanda. My mom didn't know how to turn off her emotional reactions, so she confronted Amanda with tough questions all the time. Because of this, they very seldom got along.

After a few minutes of arguing and not understanding what had actually happened, my mom eventually turned to me and asked if I could talk to Amanda.

"Amanda, what's going on? Why are you in the hospital?" I asked in frustration.

"I don't know, Nicole! Just let me talk to Mom, please."

I heard a nurse ask her a question in the background.

"Amanda, can I ask the nurse a question?"

Surprisingly, Amanda handed her the phone.

"Can you tell me why my sister is there? I am trying to help my mom understand what's going on," I said.

She paused and whispered to Amanda, "Can I tell her?"

I heard Amanda respond with a loud no.

Before the nurse could say anything else, I quickly asked, "Did you run any lab work and find drugs in her system? Did she overdose?"

Again, I heard her ask Amanda for permission to tell me. And once again, Amanda responded no.

"I'm sorry, but I do not have the permission to tell you that," the nurse responded politely.

I sighed in frustration. "Okay, thank you for trying."

I was frustrated with trying to help my mom—and Amanda, too, for that matter—yet having no idea of exactly what happened.

The nurse handed the phone back to Amanda. I again asked her what happened. She shouted at me, "Nicole, just let me talk to Mom, okay?!?"

I wasn't in the mood to argue with her and needed to go check on Christopher, who was downstairs in the living room watching TV. I gave the phone back to my mom and said, "I have no idea what's going on, but she only wants to talk to you."

My mom eventually appeared in the living room after talking to Amanda. She motioned for me to join her in the kitchen so Christopher wouldn't hear what she was going to say.

"Well, I guess she is being admitted to the hospital. She won't really tell me exactly why, but it's the psychiatric unit."

I rolled my eyes. "She must have overdosed. I kept asking the nurse, but Amanda wouldn't let her tell me why she was there. Why would she need to hide it if it wasn't drug-related?"

"I have no idea, Nicole. But I need to drive out there and bring her some things because she's going to be there for a week or so."

"Oh, wow. Well, I certainly wasn't expecting this. I'll watch Christopher or whatever you need." My mom nodded her head in agreement and then hurried upstairs to get ready.

An hour later, my mom left for the hospital to take Amanda some clothing and toiletries. Throughout the course of the day, we started to learn more details about what had happened the night before. My dad called and told me he needed to drive to Bloomsburg, a town located about an hour from where we lived. He said, "The police just called me about Amanda's car. They took it to an impound, and I need to go get it. I'll call you when I know more."

A few hours later, I heard from my dad. "Apparently, Amanda and Shannon were sitting in a grocery store parking lot last night for over three hours with the car idling and slowly creeping forward. Someone eventually called the cops, who found them. Amanda ODed in the passenger seat, and Shannon was asleep in the driver's seat with her foot on the brake. I'm going to kill her, Nicole. How could she do this? She just got out of rehab."

"Oh my god. You've gotta be kidding me. I knew she had overdosed when she called this morning from the hospital. She wouldn't tell me what happened, but why else would she have been in the hospital?"

"Well, that's what happened. And now I'm stuck paying her fucking fine, too. Had to do that before they'd give me the car. What a joke. And you know what else they found? *Tons* of stolen clothes and shoes in the trunk of her car."

"What?!"

"Yeah, apparently they're shoplifting now, too. I'm sick to my stomach, Nicole. What am I supposed to do with all this stuff?"

"I guess take it back to the store? Do you know where it's from?"

"No clue. There are no receipts because they stole all this crap."

"Right. I didn't think of that."

"I don't know what we're going to do with her, Nicole. See how much rehab helped? She is worse off now. Especially with this girl she's hanging out with."

"I know. I don't even know what to say. Mom went to take her things to the hospital. I guess she is being admitted to their psych ward. Hopefully that will help since rehab apparently didn't."

"I wouldn't count on it. I'll call you later."

Amanda had never shoplifted in her life—at least not that I was aware of. This experience showed us the reality of what can happen after your loved one is discharged from rehab. You like to believe that everyone has the best intentions and is committed to recovery. However, the harsh reality is that some people are just there because they have to be. This was the case for both Amanda and Shannon. I was not prepared for Amanda to reach this new level of shoplifting for drug money, but that's exactly what happened. She went to rehab to get better, but instead, she dove deeper in the waters of heroin use and her behaviors escalated to the next level.

I spent the day looking after Christopher while my parents each played their part in cleaning up Amanda's mess from the night before. All of this was so exhausting. I tried my best to be there for Christopher and act like everything was okay. This was so hard, though. Both my parents were struggling, and I felt so many emotions at once. How could Amanda do this again? She came home from rehab on Tuesday and overdosed just *three days later*. What was the point of even going to rehab? And what do we do now?

When Amanda had agreed to go to rehab, I remember feeling like we had won a race. The hardest part was over. She admitted she had a problem, wanted to get better, and was putting in the work to do so. Little did I know that the success rate of acute inpatient programs is very low. Half the battle is getting the person into treatment, but the most important part starts after the person gets *out* of treatment. I had no idea that my sister would come home from rehab *worse* than she went in, but that is exactly what happened.

Before going to rehab, Amanda had just started experimenting with heroin. She had gotten her feet wet and wasn't quite ready to dry off. She told me years later, "I only went to rehab because you wanted me to. I'd just started using heroin. It was a new drug to me, and I had no intention of stopping." Of course, at the time I didn't know she felt this way. I couldn't understand why she would waste twenty-eight days of her life in a program to get better, only to come out and do exactly what had gotten her in there in the first place. But you see, I still didn't understand addiction, just as I hadn't understood when she started with the pills years before. To this day, I *still* don't fully understand, to be honest. Because whatever switch did not flip on inside of Amanda's brain telling her "it's time to stop" has *always* flipped on inside of my brain.

In high school and college, I partied, just like most other people do. I drank alcohol on the weekends and experimented with weed and even some pills. But the next day, I never woke up with that *hunger* or *pull* for the drug. I don't even know what that would feel like. I partied, I had fun, and I moved on. I wish I could say my sister was able to do the same, but unfortunately, the aftermath of her first stint in rehab and subsequent relapse is only just the beginning of her story.

CHAPTER 3

THE MAKING OF A MONSTER

After her second overdose in the passenger seat of her car, in February 2014, Amanda stayed in the hospital for a few weeks to receive inpatient psychiatric care. I'm not exactly sure why she was admitted from the emergency department, and at this point, I'll never know. But for whatever reason, she qualified for an inpatient psychiatric stay after her overdose, and somehow the hospital staff convinced her to agree to it.

When Amanda was released from the hospital a few weeks later, my mom drove about an hour to pick her up. Amanda told my mom that Shannon had been arrested after the cops found them in the parking lot and begged her to pick Shannon up from jail. Apparently, Amanda and Shannon had been communicating regularly throughout this time and planned on reuniting when both were released. Shannon had been in jail while Amanda was in the hospital and was released earlier on the day of Amanda's discharge. This was not the first time Shannon had been arrested; she had been in and out of jail quite frequently, actually. From what I understand, this was mostly due to drug-related charges. Shannon was a good person deep down, but she had been intensely controlled by her opiate addiction since long before she ever met Amanda.

My mom, being the enabler she was at the time, agreed to get Shannon from jail and drove them both back to my sister's apartment. They both swore they were "done with heroin" and were going to get jobs and get their lives back together. Amanda said she wasn't going to jeopardize being there for Christopher by overdosing again and promised us she was done using heroin "for real this time." She enrolled herself back in outpatient counseling on her own volition and started looking for jobs.

Soon after her return home, Amanda revealed that she and Shannon were in a romantic relationship together. This was interesting to learn because Amanda had never before expressed a romantic interest in women. My family was skeptical, especially given their history of meeting in rehab and Amanda's subsequent overdose just three days after their discharge. How could this be a healthy relationship? They both struggled with substance abuse and had relapsed together the very day they were released from rehab. From our perspective, they couldn't separate this relationship from wanting to use drugs together. However, we were open and willing to accept their relationship if they both truly wanted to be together and could bring out the best in each other. The latter had yet to be determined.

Christopher continued to live with us at my mom's house for a while. We didn't trust Amanda after she got home, especially with Shannon staying with her. It wasn't that we didn't like Shannon; we didn't even know her. We just didn't like them *together*. We worried that if one were to relapse again, the other would as well. We couldn't see a path where they could both stay sober while spending the majority of their time together.

To our surprise, however, by early March 2014, they both had proved to be serious about recovery. Amanda continued going to both outpatient drug counseling and mental health counseling and started coming around our family more often. Shannon landed herself a job doing factory work, and Amanda started to look for a part-time job as well. Amanda also started making a greater effort with Christopher and appeared to be doing well enough to take care of him again, at least part time. She hadn't had any new incidents, and her interactions with Christopher were appropriate every time we saw her. She eventually asked to have Christopher live with her again, but we weren't convinced she was ready for that just yet. We allowed Amanda to spend more time with Christopher, and even watch him without our supervision for short periods, but he continued living with us at my mom's house.

Overall, both Amanda and Shannon were doing much better since Amanda's psychiatric hospitalization and Shannon's short-term stint in jail. They promised they were committed to a life in recovery, and they had a few months without any concerning incidents. I wish I could say this lasted and they lived happily ever after and rehabilitated, but unfortunately, just a month later, we were back to more drama.

If they were *actually clean* during this time period, at some point, they relapsed. We found out that this happened after the fact, and not because Amanda freely admitted to it. It never worked that way. Instead, we learned of their relapse when Amanda called my mom from a police station after they had been in a single-vehicle car accident on April 21, 2014.

Amanda and Shannon were driving on the interstate on their way to pick up drugs. (Shannon told me this years later; we were not aware at the time that they were picking up drugs.) They had Christopher with them in the back seat, as he was off school that day and Amanda wanted to watch him. Amanda lost control of her vehicle and veered off the side of the road, slamming into the guardrail. She later claimed, "I was reaching for my lighter on the floor and lost control of my car." She ended up totaling her vehicle. Luckily, no one was injured and no other cars were involved.

The drama did not end there. After the accident, Amanda and Shannon started physically fighting with each other alongside the interstate while Christopher stood by, watching. The fighting was so bad that passersby called the police out of concern. The police eventually arrived and arrested them both for disorderly conduct. Amanda and Shannon sat at the police station for several hours, still accompanied by six-year-old Christopher.

I learned about all of this while I was working, of course. My mom called me, upset and unsure of what to do once again. After I finished work, I decided to drive to the police station to check out the situation and, at the very least, take Christopher home with me.

I walked into the station and found the three of them sitting there; Amanda and Shannon were charged but not detained. They were simply stuck there without a vehicle and waiting for a ride. Christopher jumped out of his chair and ran to give me a hug. He must have been so confused as to what was going on. It was clear right away that Amanda was not in a good mood. She stood up and said, "Well, thank *god* someone finally came. Let's go, Shannon." She motioned toward the door as if I was supposed to immediately take the three of them home.

"What happened? Are you guys in trouble?" I asked.

"I don't know, Nicole. I lost control of my car. It's totaled. Can you just take us home?"

"I'll take you and Christopher, but I'm sorry, I don't think it's a good idea for me to take Shannon. I think you need some time apart."

"Are you fucking kidding me, Nicole? We have been sitting here for hours, and now you're going to pull this shit? C'mon, Shannon." She once again motioned toward the door as if I was kidding and would be taking them both with me.

"I'm sorry, Amanda. But *no*. I know there's more to this story, and I don't think the two of you are good for each other."

"Oh, you gotta be fucking kidding me. You're just going to leave us here?"

"No, I said I would take you and Christopher. I'm just not taking Shannon with me."

"Whatever, Nicole. Just go, then. I'm not leaving Shannon."

"Okay, that's your choice, then."

"I can't believe you, Nicole. This is fucking ridiculous. UGGGHHHH." She started shouting. I was over it.

Amanda carried on for quite a while. She wasn't used to hearing the word "no" and had become accustomed to all of us enabling her. It felt weird for me to say no, too, but I listened to my gut and what I felt was right. I knew no one would benefit from this situation continuing. And in no way was I obligated to take her or Shannon with me. The fact that she felt immediately entitled to this just shows how much we all did for her.

After a few minutes, I grew tired of listening to her, so I gathered myself and Christopher and left the police station. I held his hand as we walked out to the car and apologized for raising my voice inside. He looked at me with concerned eyes and said, "Where is my mommy? Is she coming with us?" This broke my heart. I stopped walking and leaned over to him. "It'll be okay, buddy. I promise. She's just being a bit stubborn right now. We'll have some fun at Grammy's. I'll even let you play on my phone." He smiled. "Okay, Aunt Nicki."

After this incident, things only got worse. Christopher continued staying with us at my mom's because Amanda was clearly not ready to have him back despite her "best efforts" the previous month. Her behaviors were spiraling out of control, and the sister I once knew was beginning to fade away. Almost immediately after her accident, she started showing up at my mom's house unannounced and demanding money, or cigarettes, or money for cigarettes. My mom's house was the closest place for her to walk to from her apartment, and since she no longer had a vehicle, this became a regular occurrence.

She would show up at all hours of the day, looking disheveled, sometimes with Shannon and sometimes by herself. My mom didn't know what to do or how to handle her. Amanda was out of control and had lost all sense of what was socially acceptable, or right or wrong, and had certainly lost respect for my mom and the rest of our family. She was a wrecking ball full of entitlement wreaking havoc on anyone and everyone that stood in her way. I worried that each new incident would eventually destroy my family. I wanted to protect my mom, and the worse my sister got, the more I felt the need to insert myself.

This was probably the scariest and most vulnerable time for my family. Amanda was simply out of control and turning into a monster we couldn't tame. We had no idea what to do with her and were desperate for help. We couldn't reason with her because she wasn't mentally right, but we didn't know what to do to get her the help she needed either. What I learned from this situation is that things will often get worse before they get better. And sometimes you must do whatever is necessary to shut down an escalating situation. Amanda's behaviors were spiraling out of control, and we had to go to extreme measures to intervene and finally get her the help she needed.

One afternoon, just two days after her accident, Amanda and Shannon showed up to the house and immediately started carrying on and making demands for money and cigarettes. My stepdad, Keith, began questioning them outside the house and did not want them to come inside. They got into an altercation that ended with Shannon striking Keith in the face during their attempts to get into the house. Keith called the cops, and Amanda and Shannon were both charged with disorderly conduct, yet again.

Then, a day or two later, Amanda showed up unannounced. I was upstairs in my bedroom with Christopher, and we had just turned on the movie *Frozen*. We had barely gotten ten minutes into the movie when I heard the chaos downstairs. I told Christopher to stay upstairs and watch the movie and that I would be right back. When I got downstairs and entered the kitchen, I found my sister in sweatpants and an oversized winter coat, wearing only a bra underneath. She looked like she hadn't brushed her hair or showered in days.

Next thing I knew, she started screaming at the top of her lungs: "Give me money for a pack of cigarettes. I'm not leaving until I get money for cigarettes!" My mom stood there in shock from witnessing Amanda's theatrics and appearance. I don't remember how long this went on, but I knew I needed to get Amanda out of there. I told her to leave numerous times, but she wouldn't. I became so frustrated that I screamed in her face, "Get the fuck out of here, Amanda!" The next thing I knew, Amanda lunged forward at me, and we were on the floor fighting.

Amanda and I had never fought like this in our lives, but there we were, rolling around on the kitchen floor while my mom screamed and begged us to stop. I remember thinking how weak Amanda felt and that if I wanted to, I could really hurt her. I had to hold myself back from actually hitting her, even though at that moment, it was all I wanted to do. After a minute of scuffling and rolling around, I decided to end the situation. I felt horrible hearing my mom cry and beg us to stop fighting. I ran upstairs and grabbed ten dollars from my purse. I shoved the ten-dollar bill at Amanda and told her to get the fuck out and leave us alone. Before I could blink my eyes, she had run out the back door.

It was hard to believe this nightmare was our reality. One minute I'm watching a movie with my nephew, the next I'm rolling around on my mom's floor fighting with my sister. Dealing with Amanda's antics was beginning to affect our everyday lives. We had no idea what was going to come next. We were like sitting ducks, waiting on her next move to harass us, attack us, or do whatever it took to get money from us. I couldn't handle this life anymore. I had to do something to get her under control.

After she left, I decided to call the cops and see if there was anything they could do to help us. We were being harassed on a daily basis, and who knew what the hell Amanda and Shannon were up to when they weren't harassing us? The way they were acting, I figured they had to be getting into some sort of trouble elsewhere, so maybe they were already on the police's radar.

The cops arrived at the house a few minutes later and said they had seen Shannon asleep on a bench earlier that day but didn't have enough to arrest her. They said they would keep an eye out for Shannon and Amanda and suggested that we look into getting Amanda evaluated for a psychiatric hospitalization, since she was clearly a threat to us. We hadn't considered this option, but it made sense. I didn't care which way we had to do it: whether she was in jail or a psychiatric hospital, I was desperate and just wanted Amanda contained. She was unstable, out of control, and no longer resembled the sister I once knew.

These antics went on for a few more days before we had any sort of resolution. Amanda started leaving my mom accidental voicemails on which we could hear her and Shannon physically fighting in the background. She also sent my mom several alarming text messages, including one threatening to kill herself. I decided to reach out to a crisis worker, hoping we had enough to "302" her, or what we refer to in Pennsylvania as committing someone to an involuntary psychiatric hospitalization.

I spoke with the county delegate and learned that acting out physically and emotionally while under the influence of drugs is not enough to be committed under a 302. However, if a person is threatening to harm themselves or others, you have enough to file the petition. Thankfully, my sister had helped me out with that part after sending my mom those concerning text messages threatening to harm herself.

The county delegate met with me at work so I could fill out the paperwork and explain in writing that my sister was a clear and present danger to herself and others based on her actions over the last thirty days. After filing the paperwork, I learned that the next step would be the police going to my sister's apartment to take her to the ER for a psychiatric evaluation, which they could do without a warrant under a 302 petition. If the mental health evaluators in the ER found her to be a threat to herself or others, they would then admit her for psychiatric treatment and could keep her involuntarily for up to 120 hours.

I can still feel the knot in the pit of my stomach after the county delegate left that day. I wondered if I had done the right thing. It's crazy how much guilt is involved in being a family member of someone with addiction. I honestly didn't know what other options I had, but I dreaded the backlash and guilt trip that would be coming my way. I knew that Amanda would throw all kinds of words at me to make me feel like a terrible person. She would call me a backstabber, say I betrayed her, say I don't know the meaning of family. I was scared for what was coming, but deep down I knew I did the right thing.

Amanda was terrorizing us; we were desperate and out of solutions. At this point, we had taken her son. We tried to cut her off, but she kept showing up to the house unannounced and demanding things from us, even physically fighting us to get them. It was a hopeless feeling, and we needed to take advantage of any opportunity to get her help, by whatever means necessary, because she wasn't going to do any of it willingly. I had to see beyond the guilt—getting her the help she needed was more important.

A few hours later, the cops arrived at Amanda's apartment, and the backlash started almost immediately. She didn't want to answer the door, but luckily, under the 302, the police didn't need a warrant to come inside; they had been court-ordered to pick her up. She called both me and my mom, screaming and carrying on about what we had done. She came down extra hard on me because she knew I had filed the petition. However, after her initial freak-out, the cops finally got her to go peacefully to the hospital for the psychiatric evaluation.

This is when my nerves started setting in. There were so many thoughts running through my head; I didn't know what to think from one minute to the next. *What if she fakes it well enough that they don't commit her for further treatment? What if she convinces them she is fine, they let her go back home, and things are actually worse because she is extremely pissed off at us?* I tried to breathe and reminded myself that it was out of my control. I had to trust the professionals to make the right call.

A few hours later, we learned that Amanda was going to be admitted to the psychiatric unit at our local hospital. They could keep her involuntarily for up to 120 hours. After that, they could discharge her, she could voluntarily agree to stay for additional treatment, or the hospital could petition a 303, which is the next step for further involuntary treatment. We worried they would only keep her for five days if she didn't agree to further treatment. We feared her behavior would then be worse because she was so upset and pissed off that we had put her there in the first place. Nonetheless, we were thankful she was in treatment.

After a few days, to our surprise, Amanda actually came around and was thankful we had intervened. She opened up to us and admitted she needed help. She revealed that she had been abusing her prescription for Klonopin, a strong benzodiazepine that is prescribed for various reasons, most commonly to treat seizures, anxiety, and insomnia. However, when taken in excess or combined with alcohol or other drugs, it can cause paranoia, suicidal ideation, and impair memory and judgment. She said she was taking so many of these pills, she couldn't even remember how many, due to the memory impairment aspect. This is when I also learned about "benzo rage." Essentially, in some cases, benzodiazepines can actually cause a paradoxical effect, in which the person may exhibit uncharacteristic behavior with increased hostility, aggression, rage, and anger. This all made so much sense considering everything we had witnessed over the previous few weeks, in April through early May, when I filed the petition.

Amanda's abuse of her Klonopin prescription explained the outbursts, unexpected altercations at my mom's house, her car accident, and our fight in my mom's kitchen. She apologized for everything and thanked us for getting her help. She knew she needed it but was too stubborn and high on Klonopin to recognize her need. We were surprised by how well she responded to psychiatric treatment and even more surprised when she agreed to stay for additional treatment after the mandatory five days had passed.

During her hospitalization, Amanda was also diagnosed with bipolar disorder and got her medications straightened out for the first time in a while. Due to her misuse, she was no longer prescribed Klonopin. The social workers set her up with outpatient psychiatric services to follow up on her mental health issues. Overall, it looked like we were heading in the right direction. We got her mental health needs under control, and from what she told us, she hadn't been using heroin prior to the hospitalization. We thought that with good follow-up mental health and drug and alcohol counseling, she would have enough support to succeed. Unfortunately, these stories are always more complicated than that.

CHAPTER 4

2016:
THE YEAR THAT
CHANGED EVERYTHING

After Amanda was discharged from her psychiatric hospitalization in early May 2014, she finally got her life back on track. She participated in outpatient drug and alcohol and mental health counseling services for several months. She started taking an opioid antagonist medication to manage her cravings and prevent relapse. She was also prescribed lithium to manage her bipolar disorder and was no longer prescribed Klonopin for anxiety. Instead, her doctor prescribed an antidepressant to manage both her depression and anxiety symptoms, rather than the abuse-prone benzodiazepine she had been taking previously. She promised she was done with heroin and was ready to commit to her recovery, not just for herself, but also for her son. We were skeptical at first, of course, but we decided to let her prove it to us.

After a good month on her new medication regimen and attending follow-up counseling, Amanda continued to demonstrate that she had indeed changed. She had more mental clarity than we had seen from her in years. We were proud of how far she had come in just a month's time. She requested that Christopher come back and live with her again, and at this point, he really wanted to be back home. It had been almost six months since he'd started staying with us at my mom's house, and he was ready to be at home with his mommy. Amanda had also reconnected with Christopher's father regarding an unofficial custody agreement. He would start taking Christopher every other weekend starting in May as well. Based on Amanda's consistent progress and her effective mental health treatments—both medication and counseling—we decided she could have Christopher back in her custody. We were only a few minutes away and would obviously check in frequently. Christopher was absolutely thrilled to finally be going back home to his mom.

Throughout the next few months, into the summer and fall of 2014, Amanda continued to flourish. She and Christopher spent a lot of time with our family, and she appeared to be doing better than she had in years. We all had a fun summer together without any new incidents or concerns. Christopher also continued to spend time with his dad almost every other weekend throughout the summer. It appeared that Amanda was doing well on her new medications and, thankfully, was staying away from drugs—at least that we were aware of. Shannon and Amanda were still partners and living together, so we were always somewhat fearful that things could change rather quickly, but we could only go by what we saw and what they told us. They promised they were sober and gave us no reason to believe they weren't when we saw them in person. We had to learn to trust and let go.

In September 2014, I decided to move to Nashville to start a new chapter in my life. I had graduated college two years prior and had been living with my mom and stepdad while I worked at my first job as an occupational therapist. It was nice to live at home and spend time with my parents while saving money at the same time. And with everything we had been through earlier that year, I was happy that I had been home to help out with Christopher. But I was ready to move on with my life. I was twenty-five years old, single, and had a career that allowed me to find a job anywhere. I had nothing to lose, and for once, I was thinking of *myself* first, instead of my family.

On moving day, Amanda and Christopher came down to the house to say goodbye to me. We took several pictures together outside to capture some memories. It was my last day in the small town of Minersville, Pennsylvania, and I couldn't have been more ready to say goodbye. On the other hand, I knew my family was going to miss me. I prayed Amanda could hold herself together and stay healthy for her son and for our family's sake. I wasn't sure how they would be able to handle things without me. Although Amanda was doing well at the time, we knew that with opioid addiction, relapse was always a possibility in the future.

Moving to Nashville turned out to be the best decision I'd ever made. Just a few days after moving, I met a few friends who are still some of my very best friends to this day. A few months later, I met the man who would eventually become my husband. Taking that chance and putting myself first felt foreign to me after taking care of my family for so many years. But I knew they would be okay; they would have to be.

After I moved, Amanda continued making good decisions and slowly earned my parents' trust back. She completed outpatient drug counseling and landed a part-time job at a local tobacco shop. By March 2015, my parents trusted her enough to help her get a new vehicle (if you remember, she had totaled the last one). My mom and dad decided it would be best for Amanda to have a car so she could get to work and take Christopher to appointments and school. They agreed to give Amanda my mom's old car and split the cost of her monthly car insurance payments, which weren't cheap, due to her driving history.

From March through December 2015, Amanda demonstrated more responsibility for herself than she had in years. She maintained primary custody of Christopher, with his dad seeing him occasionally on weekends. Amanda also continued working at her part-time job and seemed to have a good relationship with Shannon. She kept in touch with me from time to time, which always meant that she was doing okay. While I wasn't thrilled about her relationship with Shannon, I tried to be as accepting as I could.

We thought the worst part was over. Maybe Amanda had learned from her mistakes and was heading in the right direction. After all, she had completed her outpatient drug counseling and was still seeing a mental health therapist regularly. What more could we ask for?

Unfortunately, like most families affected by opioid addiction, there was a lot going on that we didn't know about. In late March 2015, a child protective services (CPS) case was opened to investigate Amanda and Christopher's living situation. We had absolutely no knowledge of this at the time and found out years later, but according to documents Amanda kept, "the agency received concerns regarding her drug use." The documents also mentioned Christopher was "at imminent risk to be removed from his home and placed in foster care absent preventative effective services." Christopher's father was informed of this investigation via mail according to the documentation, but he did not seek increased custody of Christopher at the time. According to the outlined family service plan, Amanda needed to comply with random drug screenings, participate in outpatient drug treatment, and cooperate with unannounced home visits by CPS caseworkers. Eventually, the investigation was dropped, and the case was closed in October 2015. Amanda was compliant and apparently had met all the criteria to maintain custody of her son.

Several months later, however, without the close eyes of CPS holding her accountable, Amanda must have relapsed. On New Year's Day, 2016, my family very quickly learned that Amanda was not doing as well as we had thought.

On that January 1, Amanda got into another car accident. She had just dropped Christopher off at a family friend's house and was heading back to her place when she veered off the side of the road, went over the guardrail and down a hill, and completely destroyed the rear door behind the driver's seat. Thankfully, there were no other cars involved. The accident was 100 percent caused by her losing control of the vehicle.

When the EMTs arrived, Amanda refused any medical attention. She insisted she was fine and just wanted to go home. I found this suspicious. Why would she refuse medical care if she was clean and sober? What did she have to hide? This didn't make sense to me, but it seemed like she had just gotten away with another DWI. Amanda denied any wrongdoing to my family and swore she hadn't taken any drugs. My parents said, "She claims she simply lost control of her car and isn't sure how it happened." Years later, she eventually admitted to taking a large concoction of pills before getting behind the wheel. But at the time, she didn't dare tell us the truth.

I now consider this wreck a premonition of what was to come in 2016, or what I call *the year that changed everything*. After her car accident, Amanda slowly started unraveling and outwardly regressing into her old patterns. Although I lived in Nashville, I knew from everything my parents told me that she was not doing well. We didn't know the severity at the time because Amanda always denied being on drugs and lied about everything. But as the months went on, it became clear she was struggling to hold it together.

Even though she denied her drug use, Amanda always had certain "tells." Her attitude would completely change. She would become angry and frustrated easily. She would stop calling to catch up or to talk about nothing in particular. Instead, she would only call when she needed something, and if you told her no, she would either hang up immediately or get angry and pick a fight. She became an intolerable person to deal with unless you gave her whatever she wanted or didn't ask her any tough questions. She was barely talking to me, so I knew from that alone that she was probably not in a good place.

As time went by and these patterns continued, I knew it wouldn't be long before I heard from my parents that Amanda had done something *really* bad. I expected to find out at any time that she had lost her job, got caught using heroin, or *worse*, overdosed. I started to hear frequently from my mom about how upset she was with Amanda. The calls became more regular, and I was always the sounding board. One day, she was pissed off because Amanda was asking her for money, and she didn't know how Amanda was blowing through her paychecks so quickly. Another time, she was upset because Amanda needed a ride to work, but when she went to pick Amanda up, she was still asleep. The writing was on the wall, but my mom continued to believe that Amanda was sober because Amanda *insisted* she was.

However, by April 2016, just a few months after the accident, Amanda couldn't hide it anymore. She had started using heroin again, and she could never hide that like she could when she was popping pills. Recall from my story in the introduction that about a week or so into April, my mom had called me, hysterical. She had just found Amanda and her friend Mitch on the floor at Amanda's apartment after they had done heroin and "fallen out." In opioid-use terms, "falling out," or losing consciousness shortly after using heroin, is essentially the precursor to overdosing. Sometimes opioid users "fall out" and you cannot wake them up like my mom was able to that day in Amanda's apartment. Sometimes "falling out" leads to overdose and the only way to arouse the person is by administering Narcan. In this case, both Amanda and Mitch were lucky that my mom had found them when she did and that she was able to wake them up.

After that day, we should have known better. We should have expected the worst given Amanda's history with heroin. But we were still so ignorant and naive when it came to addiction. We didn't understand the hold heroin and strong opioids have over people. My family also tended to look the other way when they saw red flags, instead of investigating deeper. Even though my mom knew Amanda had done heroin that day, she didn't remove Christopher from Amanda's home. Amanda swore she wasn't using "like that" and even went to work later that day. My mom decided to give her another chance despite her better judgment. Needless to say, this wasn't the right call, but unfortunately, we cannot rewrite history. We weren't prepared for the reality check that followed, which proved just how scary heroin can be.

I'll never forget the date of Amanda's next overdose. It was April 15, 2016—the day before her thirty-second birthday. It was just starting to feel like springtime in Nashville: warm enough to sit outside but not feel like you're completely melting from the heat and humidity of summer. I got off work and said to Cort, my now husband and then boyfriend, "Let's go sit on a patio somewhere and drink margaritas." He was excited because we both love margaritas and tacos.

We chose Taco Mamacita, one of our favorite local spots. When we arrived, we had to wait for a table because apparently everyone else had the same idea. While we were waiting at the bar and enjoying a margarita, I got a call from my mom. I didn't think much of it, and it was noisy, so I didn't answer. My mom texted me immediately after: "It's urgent, call me back."

That's when the panic set in. I knew it had to be about my sister; this was only a week after the call from my mom telling me she had found Amanda and Mitch on the floor of Amanda's apartment.

I walked out to the parking lot and called my mom back. She quickly filled me in on everything that was happening. "Nicole, Amanda has overdosed. Christopher found her on the floor and couldn't wake her up. He texted me and said, 'Grammy can you come to my house? I can't wake my mommy up.' I'm heading there right now. I'll keep you updated on what's going on."

All of a sudden, everything just stopped; the moment is seared into my memory forever. I struggled to process what my mom had just said, but I knew I couldn't go back into that restaurant. How could I go about my life and act like everything was okay while my sister's life hung in the balance? I canceled our plans and waited to hear back from my mom.

Cort and I walked out to the car and sat there for a while. I couldn't believe what my mom had just told me. How could Amanda do this *again*? And with eight-year-old Christopher *in the house*? I was worried and upset, but furious at the same time. How could Christopher go through more of this? He deserved so much better.

I decided to call my dad and fill him in. I was hesitant to call him at first because my dad tended to retreat whenever things got bad with Amanda. He never wanted to be involved at this point because he couldn't handle the stress. Long before Amanda had ever tried heroin, she lived with him for years while she casually abused Vicodin, Percocet, Xanax, and Suboxone. He had basically raised Christopher for the first few years of his life, once Amanda's Vicodin addiction was in full force. After she started using heroin, anytime her issues escalated, he just shut down. He didn't want to know details; he couldn't handle them anymore. But this time was different. We didn't know if she was going to live or die. We didn't know how bad her overdose was or what she had taken. All we knew was that she was unconscious, and Christopher was the one who had found her.

My dad took the news as best he could. He didn't say much, of course. He was a man of few words when it came to this stuff. But he told me he was going to call out of work because he couldn't stand the thought of being on the road worried about her. My dad was a truck driver and worked third shift his entire life. While everyone else was sleeping, he spent his nights driving and worrying about all kinds of things. Unfortunately, he would be worrying a lot more tonight, but at least he could be at home.

My mom called me a few minutes later with some updates. She and my stepdad, Keith, got to Amanda's apartment and found her on the floor. She was breathing very slowly, and her lips and face looked blue. My mom called 911 immediately. Keith removed Christopher from the home and took him to their house while my mom waited for the ambulance to arrive. The EMTs arrived quickly—within seven minutes—but by the time they got there, Amanda's respirations were down to four per minute. This was all my mom knew when she called. The EMTs weren't very optimistic that Amanda was going to make it; her respiratory system was shutting down.

The EMTs quickly prepared Amanda to be medevaced to a nearby hospital for emergency care. When they got her to the helicopter pad, they finally administered Narcan, which immediately shot her back to life. The EMTs quickly realized they wouldn't need to medevac her to the hospital, but still recommended she be taken to the local ER via ambulance. However, just as she had after her car accident a few months prior, Amanda refused all medical care. So instead of heading to the hospital, she was taken to the police station to be processed on charges for reckless endangerment and endangering the welfare of a child. Afterward, one of Amanda's friends picked her up, and she went back home for the night.

While all of this was going on, I anxiously waited in our apartment while my mom relayed the details. As the events continued to unfold throughout the night, I was completely mind-blown by the entire situation. The whole night felt surreal. There was no way that in a matter of a few hours, Amanda went from nearly dying as her respiratory system shut down to going back home at the end of night like nothing had ever happened. Did Narcan really work that effectively? Her respirations were down to four per minute, so the oxygen getting to her brain had to be minimal. What were the repercussions of that? We would never know, as Amanda again avoided medical evaluation and treatment.

The next day, Amanda went about her life as usual. My mom and Keith agreed to keep Christopher at their house until we could figure out a long-term plan. We were all upset about what had happened, and we didn't understand how things had gotten so bad so quickly. We never thought she would use around Christopher, but we were obviously ignorant to the reality of Amanda's situation. Of course, at the time, we didn't know how frequently Amanda was using heroin or the severity of her substance abuse. Everything she had told us had been a lie. I've since learned that when opioid addiction is that bad, the person with the addiction loses control over their choices. Even though, deep down, Amanda probably knew she shouldn't use around Christopher, she didn't have the willpower or executive functioning to look past those strong cravings. But we didn't understand this at the time, so this was surprising and scary for all of us.

I was frustrated and angry with Amanda, but I knew I had to help my family. I called her and begged her to go to rehab. She laughed me off and quickly shut down the idea of rehab. She barked at me over the phone, "It was a one-time thing, Nicole. I used the wrong stuff. I won't use it again. I'm done with that stuff. And honestly, there's nothing they can teach me at rehab that I don't already know." It was the same old song and dance once again, and she was nowhere near ready to admit she had a problem.

I didn't feel like fighting with her, and it wasn't my responsibility to convince her to go. As hard as it was to accept, I knew I couldn't force her to do anything. The silver lining in the situation was that the police were now involved. She had been charged with reckless endangerment and endangering the welfare of a child. So even though I couldn't make her go back to rehab, I thought the fear of going to jail might be enough motivation for her to choose to go. These charges wouldn't necessarily land her in jail, but she would most likely face probation and would have to stay clean to meet her probation requirements.

Honestly, it was hard to believe that these were the first major charges against her since she had started using heroin just over two years ago, in 2014. We had no idea how much Christopher had witnessed over the last few years living in the house with Amanda and Shannon. We thought we could trust her and believed her when she said she wasn't using, especially after completing drug counseling and starting opioid antagonist medication. From the outside, things had seemed okay up until my mom had found Amanda and Mitch passed out on the floor, less than a week before Amanda's overdose.

Even then, my mom didn't quite comprehend the severity of Amanda's addiction. None of us did. I mean, how could I truly understand when I was living out of state and relying on what my parents were telling me? My mom obviously didn't want to see what was really happening and always believed Amanda, even when the truth was staring her in the face.

Regardless, I was proud of my mom for acting quickly and remaining calm while handling Amanda's overdose, and especially for removing Christopher from the house right away. I learned that although my mom always claimed she "couldn't take the stress" of dealing with Amanda, when push came to shove, she handled everything better than anyone could have expected.

I also learned that whatever the hell Narcan was, it was a fucking lifesaver. I didn't know how many times Amanda had overdosed up to this point, but I did know that every time she survived, Narcan had saved her life. I get upset when I see social media posts hating on Narcan being handed out for free in communities as part of overdose-death prevention initiatives. The people writing these posts claim that free Narcan only encourages drug use, but being a family member of someone with opioid addiction, I see it completely differently in that *it saves lives*. I know the Narcan haters on Facebook wouldn't be bitching about free Narcan if their sisters had almost died. I can guarantee that.

It wasn't until this overdose, in April 2016, that we started to open our eyes and understand what it means to love someone with opioid addiction. My family learned that we couldn't trust a word that came out of Amanda's mouth. We also learned that she was in *much deeper* than she had ever led us to believe, and it was going to take *a lot* to recover the girl we once knew.

CHAPTER 5

THE AFTERMATH

In the years before Amanda's first heroin overdose in 2014, she always told me she'd never try heroin. She was emphatic about that. She swore it was a "dirty drug," and if I ever found out she was using it, I should know she was in a really bad place. Yet here we were, just over two years later, and it was clear that she was in over her head with heroin. Remember, 2015 had been a relatively good year (at least from what we knew), and 2016 was the year that changed everything.

On April 15, 2016, the night Amanda overdosed for at least the third time (we didn't know the exact number because she may have hidden some from us), Christopher was outside playing with his friends. It was early evening, and Amanda knew Christopher would be coming in soon, so she shot up with enough time to clean up before he came inside. Obviously, this didn't work out for her, as we know he found her overdosed and unconscious on the floor. Amanda later claimed the heroin she shot up was laced with fentanyl, a synthetic opioid even more powerful than heroin, which caused her to immediately overdose. Assuming the heroin had not been laced with fentanyl, Amanda planned to go about her night as usual, including taking care of Christopher when he came inside from playing.

Although hard to imagine, not all "heroin highs" resemble what we see in the movies, where a person uses and then slumps over in a chair or starts nodding off. From what I have learned over the years after watching my sister go through this, people essentially use opioids for two reasons: (1) for the euphoric effects to numb their pain and/or anxiety, or (2) to avoid being dope sick.

"Dope sick" is the term used to describe the excruciating symptoms of opioid withdrawal. This usually sets in about six to twelve hours after a person last uses their drug of choice and peaks within three to four days. The physical symptoms are similar to those of the flu and include vomiting, diarrhea, hot and cold flashes, body aches, sensations of bugs crawling underneath the skin, insomnia, and profuse sweating. These physical symptoms are coupled with mental and emotional symptoms, including agitation, anxiety, paranoia, depression, and despondency. Opioid users live their day-to-day lives with the goal of avoiding dope sickness at all costs. In order to do this, a person may go to extreme measures to get their next fix, including lying, stealing, or even prostitution.

Dope sickness is often the reason for relapse and fatal overdoses after relapse when a person is using abstinence alone in their treatment plan. This is why it's important for opioid users to not only follow through with long-term drug counseling or a twelve-step program, but to also consider medication-assisted treatment (MAT), such as methadone, Suboxone, buprenorphine, or naltrexone to reduce cravings and withdrawal symptoms, especially in the early stages of treatment. Historically, there have been some misconceptions about these medications, with some people claiming that this form of treatment simply replaces one substance use disorder with another. There was definitely a time I thought this as well. However, these medications affect people who have developed a high tolerance to opioids differently in that they don't produce euphoric effects. In addition, studies have shown MAT reduces the risk of overdose death by up to 50 percent. These medications reduce cravings, eliminate withdrawal symptoms, and may even allow opioid users to function normally again, including attending school or resuming work. The long-term goal is to eventually be weaned off these medications, but some may stay on these for years before it is appropriate to do this or may even take these medications for the rest of their lives.

Amanda had utilized MAT, including both Suboxone and methadone, intermittently throughout the years, even dating back to her pre-heroin days. I remember coming home from college and seeing her at my dad's house taking her sublingual Suboxone like clockwork. She never missed a dose and relied heavily on it to manage her chronic pain as well as opioid cravings, as she had been highly addicted to narcotic painkillers prior to starting Suboxone. In 2014, Amanda started methadone after she completed her inpatient psychiatric treatment and participated in outpatient drug counseling. This had been working for her for a while until she relapsed sometime in March 2015. As I previously mentioned, my family wasn't aware of this relapse, but we later found out she had to comply with CPS in order to maintain custody of Christopher, and she obviously found a way to stay clean again, because that case was closed in October 2015. However, sometime between then and this overdose in April 2016, she had relapsed and started using heroin yet again.

I'll never know what it's like to be high on heroin, so writing about this is hard for me because I can't fully comprehend what my sister was going through. I didn't understand why Amanda kept relapsing, and at the time, it was hard for me to have sympathy for her. Why couldn't she stay sober for her son? How many different treatments did she need? And why couldn't she stick to any of them? None of it made any sense to me.

From what I understand now, though, using opioids "flips a switch" in the brain and produces a euphoria that numbs any pain and suffering the user may be experiencing. This is often why many opioid users start in the first place: they are simply looking for an escape. For some, the pain might be from an early childhood trauma, which doesn't need to be a "big trauma." Emotional trauma in early childhood is all about one's perception of their needs being unmet. Over time, when emotional and attachment needs are perceived to be unmet, individuals can develop nervous system changes as they assume a chronic state of "fight or flight." These changes can trigger a neurological predisposition to addiction and addictive behaviors. For others the trigger could be trauma that occurred later in life but still brings on the same emotional avoidance that leads to addiction. Using opioids becomes the easy "on/off switch" for the person dealing with emotional trauma. And then the drug use itself brings on feelings of shame and guilt, which only exacerbates this vicious cycle. Essentially, opioid users eventually start *using more* to turn off the pain and guilt they carry around from *using to begin with.*

For years Amanda used heroin and opioids as a crutch to stop herself from feeling any pain or the emotional triggers she carried around. In her junior year of high school, Amanda went through a difficult time after losing several close friends in a bad car accident. She also experienced the loss of our uncle and her then boyfriend's mother, whom she was very close with, all within the same year. Going through these experiences at a vulnerable age, while she was also starting to experiment with drugs and alcohol, may have triggered changes in her brain and made her more susceptible to addiction. Again, this is hard for me to fully comprehend, as I did not live her story or walk in her shoes. I can only speak of what I know and the things I've read about over the years that have helped me better understand heroin and opioid addiction.

On the night of her overdose, I don't think Amanda suspected she would overdose from the amount of heroin she used. However, I will never be able to wrap my head around how someone can use a drug as powerful as heroin and still expect to be able to care for their child. I often think about what Christopher might have witnessed growing up in Amanda's care. Or the things he had to do for himself simply because his mommy "wasn't able" or "was too tired" or "didn't feel good." It hurts my heart knowing that my family and I could have done more for him in those years, but we were too naive and didn't fully understand the severity of my sister's addiction. We were always very involved in Christopher's life, but we should have kept a closer eye on him after he went back into Amanda's care. Maybe if we had, we could have prevented Christopher from witnessing everything he did, including finding Amanda unconscious after she had overdosed. But then again, maybe if he hadn't found her, Amanda would not have survived that night. There will always be many "what ifs" in the mind of a family member of someone with opioid addiction.

After Amanda's overdose, things were never the same for her or my family. With CPS involved, she obviously lost custody of Christopher, so he was staying with my mom and stepdad until the end of the school year. A few days after her overdose, I decided to reach out to Christopher's father and tell him what had happened. He and my sister had split up when Christopher was very young, and he hadn't been a big part of Christopher's life up until this point. Amanda and his father had a short-lived, every-other-week schedule arrangement in 2014, but for some reason, that didn't last long. Christopher would see his dad on rare occasions, but my sister was his primary caretaker for the first eight years of his life.

Not surprisingly, Christopher's father was very concerned by what I had told him. Shortly after learning the full scope of what had happened and the state Amanda was in, he filed for legal custody of Christopher. With my sister's charges pending, CPS and the court system ultimately became responsible for determining the best living situation for Christopher.

Until the school year was over, Christopher lived with my mom, and his dad visited occasionally on weekends. My mom and Christopher's dad then went to court to decide whether or not it was appropriate for Christopher to transition from living with my mom to living full-time with his dad. The judge ultimately decided that it was best to have a trial period, rather than immediately ordering Christopher to live with his dad, whom he had barely seen for the first eight years of his life. So, for the rest of that summer, Christopher went back and forth each week between my mom's house and his dad's house, and another court date was scheduled prior to the next school year to decide where he would continue to live.

While Christopher was staying with my mom, he would often ask, "Where is my mommy?" or "Is my mommy coming over today?" or "When can I see my mommy?" It was heart-breaking for my mom to have to answer these questions, which she ultimately did not know the answers to. Amanda rarely called and never came to visit. And when she did call or visit, it was always because she needed something: money, a ride some-where, or food. This did not sit well with the CPS caseworkers involved. From their point of view, Amanda had messed up in a major way, yet did not seem concerned about or even interested in her child since making this huge mistake. When they interviewed Christopher, he told them he was sad that he didn't see his mommy much anymore and that he didn't know where she was.

Continuing on her negative trend that year, Amanda was setting herself up to lose full custody of Christopher by showing no remorse and putting in zero effort to make any sort of amends for her actions. From the outside looking in, I was angry about how she was handling this situation. It seemed like she couldn't care less and was giving up on being a mom altogether. I now know this was because Amanda felt extremely guilty, and being around Christopher inten-sified that for her. She fell further into her addiction and avoided coming around because she simply couldn't handle how terrible she felt about the situation. Unfortunately, CPS didn't care about her guilt, and they were prepared to give Christopher's father full custody.

The judge and CPS caseworkers thoroughly interviewed Christopher on multiple occasions, and he verbalized wanting to live with his dad. According to their records, he told them several times he felt "okay" about living with his dad and "liked being with his dad." The judge ultimately decided that Christopher would live with his dad full-time and start the next school year where his dad lived, which was about two hours away from Amanda and the rest of my family.

My mom wasn't thrilled with the judge's decision since she had grown close to Christopher over the last few years and was going to miss seeing him every day and taking care of him. However, she understood that his dad had rights, and it was not her decision to make. So that was that. There was not much more we could do, and being so far away in Tennessee, I wasn't much of a help throughout this process.

Christopher was going to be in a much better situation than he had been when he was living with my sister. Of course, my family was sad that he would be farther away and they would not get to see him as much, but they also respected Christopher's wishes and trusted that his dad would take good care of him. My family didn't see Christopher nearly as often after this point, especially over the next year or so while Amanda struggled more with her addiction. We always reminded Christopher that no matter what happened, we were only a phone call away and would always be there for him regardless of the circumstances. I know Amanda wanted to be there for her son, too, but in order for her to do so, at some point she needed to put her life back together. This was her constant struggle.

On top of losing custody of Christopher, later in the summer of 2016, Amanda also lost her job at the tobacco shop.

On the day she was fired, she showed up to work high on both heroin and meth, which she had started using simultaneously. Amanda's friend later explained to me, "She would be down on heroin, but then need to wake up, so she would do meth and the combination of the two just completely wrecked her brain." According to her friend, Amanda started hallucinating on the job and was convinced there was a waterfall coming out of the ceiling. Freaked out, she frantically called her boss to tell him about it. When he arrived and found no such waterfall, it didn't take him long to see what was going on. He told her she needed to go home for the day.

Amanda then left the tobacco shop, walked down to another store, and within ten minutes returned to work as if the incident had never happened. Her boss looked at her in shock and asked, "What are you doing here?"

Amanda responded, "What do you mean? I'm coming in to work," as if she were going into work for the *first* time that day. At that point, her boss was not having any more of it and called the cops to escort her home.

Her friend later told me, "After Amanda got back home, she completely forgot about everything that happened and insisted that she needed a ride to work"—again, as if she had *never been there.*

This "amnesia" became a pattern for Amanda over the course of 2016 and 2017. As she continued to use both heroin and meth, it became extremely difficult for her to pretend that she wasn't high. My parents would send me videos of her while she was high and never once could I believe what I was seeing. I couldn't understand how feeling that way was even desirable. Understanding addiction is challenging when you don't experience it firsthand, and it took me a long time to recognize this.

My mom struggled to deal with my sister and would call me to complain or ask me to "handle" the situation when things got out of control, which usually meant they were fighting about something. My hands were tied most of the time because there was not much I could do while I was in Tennessee and Amanda and my entire family were in Pennsylvania. Every time my mom called me, my heart would sink. I never knew what to expect: would she tell me Amanda was dead, overdosed, or in trouble with the cops? My anxiety around the situation was growing each day as my sister continued to ghost her son and use IV drugs.

I love my family, but they put a lot of pressure on me. I felt like I was the only one capable of fixing every bad situation Amanda put us through. I hated seeing my mom upset and became extremely protective of her. This caused me to be angry at and resentful of my sister for a long time. I couldn't understand how she could put our family through these things and have no remorse and no repercussions for her actions.

This back and forth between my sister and my family continued for the rest of the summer of 2016. The stress I felt living through this without anyone to talk to was weighing more and more on me with each passing day. A close friend of mine, whose brother also struggled with addiction, shared with me that Nar-Anon meetings had been helpful for her parents and family. Nar-Anon is a twelve-step program designed to help relatives and friends of addicts recover from the effects of living with an addicted relative or friend. I had previously attended one Nar-Anon meeting with my mom when I still lived in Pennsylvania. She cried the whole time and said she would never go back. I remember crying a lot too, but it was a good cry—the cleansing kind that felt like therapy. Dealing with all of this while being separated from my family was challenging, so I thought it might be a good idea to try Nar-Anon again. If anything, I could learn some coping skills and meet some people who would also understand what I was going through.

I can't remember how many meetings I attended, probably a handful or so, but I never had the courage to speak up at any of them. However, attending and listening to others share their stories was still impactful. I learned a lot about detachment, loving without enabling, and the importance of taking care of yourself. Detachment, or the ability to "let go," allows you to see the situation in a more objective and realistic way. It teaches you that you are not responsible for the actions of the person with addiction, which is so important in releasing control over this disease. Detachment does not come easily and is best accomplished through regular attendance of Nar-Anon meetings and working with a sponsor.

I also learned about the concept of codependency, which is all too common within addiction. Codependency essentially means you become "addicted to the person with addiction." In my family, my mom was addicted to my sister, and I was addicted to my mom. I had to learn that I couldn't be the savior all the time. *I needed to put myself first and know that nothing I did or any of the worry I created in my head was going to change what my sister wanted to do.* I learned that you truly are *powerless over the person with addiction,* which would continue to be an important lesson for me in the years to come.

CHAPTER 6

ENOUGH IS ENOUGH

Much to everyone's surprise, in late July 2016, Amanda told my family she was ready to change and wanted to go back to rehab. I think a big part of this was the anticipation of her upcoming court hearings and pending charges. Remember, Amanda was facing some major charges—reckless endangerment and endangering the welfare of a child—as a result of her overdose in April, while Christopher was under her care. In Pennsylvania, endangering the welfare of a child is a crime that occurs when a parent or guardian supervising a child under eighteen years of age knowingly endangers the child by violating a duty of care, protection, or support. This is a misdemeanor of the first degree and carries a maximum penalty of five years in jail and a $10,000 fine. In addition, reckless endangerment is considered a second-degree misdemeanor in Pennsylvania, and those convicted can face up to two years in prison as well as a fine up to $5,000.

Keeping all of this in mind, we assumed her sudden change of heart was most likely due to fear of these upcoming charges and the reality that she could be facing jail time. Despite this, we were happy that she had found whatever motivation she needed to get herself back on the road to recovery. My mom and Aunt Anne Marie—my dad's sister who often helped everyone in my family, including my sister—assisted Amanda in getting set up at a new rehab facility.

I communicated with Amanda a few times while she was in rehab, and she assured me she was doing better. My parents thought so, too, and my mom even brought my grandmother there for a family visit. After spending four weeks in rehab, Amanda prepared for her discharge back home, with outpatient counseling arranged by the treatment facility. I felt nervous about her return home as I couldn't forget what had happened after the first time she exited rehab.

When Amanda called me prior to her discharge, I begged her to reconsider her discharge plans. I tried to convince her to go directly to a sober living house instead of returning home to her previous environment, where she would be in the same place and surrounded by the same people who reminded her of using. We had learned from her last experience in rehab that returning directly home is usually not the best discharge plan. I worried that she would immediately relapse like last time. The red flags were evident when she insisted on going back home to her apartment and would not agree to continue treatment in sober living. Regardless of how many times I pleaded with her to reconsider, Amanda was stubborn and there was no changing her mind.

After twenty-eight days in inpatient drug rehab, Amanda returned home and relapsed within a short period of time. To be honest, I'm not exactly sure how much time passed between her discharge and when she actually relapsed, but I know it wasn't very long. I could never really know for sure because she always lied. Her relapses always happened several weeks, if not months, before she would actually tell us. Sometimes her drug use would become so evident that she couldn't hide it any longer. I wish I could say that I didn't see this coming, but I had known it would happen the moment she decided to step back into her old environment.

The interesting thing about recovery and addiction is that relapse is expected and often necessary to take the next steps forward. According to the National Institute on Drug Abuse (NIDA), 40 to 60 percent of individuals in recovery relapse after completing treatment. This is comparable to physical illnesses like asthma and high blood pressure, which have a relapse rate of 50 to 70 percent. Because the chances of relapse after rehab are moderately high, relapse is a normal part of recovery and should not be considered an individual failure. In addition, per the NIDA, a relapse indicates that a person may need to alter their treatment plan or possibly return to inpatient treatment. For Amanda, this relapse was important because it showed her that *people*, *places*, and *things* do matter. She couldn't simply return to her old life and expect what she had just learned in twenty-eight days to stick with her. It was impossible to think this would work for anyone struggling with addiction, but you cannot force someone into recovery. They simply have to want it for themselves. I say this confidently now, but it took me a long time to learn this.

Being surrounded by the same friends and triggers, Amanda fell right back into her old patterns of behavior. Remember I've said she was stubborn? Well, she was, *especially* when it came to being in control of herself and her decisions. She never wanted to be told what to do and never wanted to answer to other people. She was determined to return home and thought she was strong enough to stay sober despite the odds being stacked against her.

For quite some time, she hid behind a facade of sobriety around my family. But she couldn't hide from me. I knew that once I started hearing from her less frequently, she was back to using. I tried to explain this to my mom, but she always wanted to believe Amanda, even when her better judgment (and her other daughter) was telling her differently. A positive from all of this was that both Amanda and my family learned something valuable from this relapse. In order to set herself up for success in recovery, she needed to be in a supportive environment with structure and ongoing follow-up care. She needed sober living, and we would never let her discharge directly home from rehab again. Of course, we knew we couldn't force her to do anything, but since my dad paid the rent for her apartment, we could end her lease while she was in treatment and give her the choice of going into sober living or being cut off financially. This was our plan going forward, and I'd highly recommend it if your loved one in recovery is dependent on your family for their living arrangements. Returning home to the same environment they've known for years, surrounded by triggers and memories of drug use, does not support successful outcomes.

In late 2016, Amanda had her court date for her charges of reckless endangerment and endangering the welfare of a child. Since this was her first offense, she was given two years' probation under what is called "the ARD program," short for Accelerated Rehabilitative Disposition program. In Pennsylvania, this program is designed for first-time offenders with no prior criminal history and is considered more rehabilitative than punitive. Individuals must be accepted into the program by the county's district attorney. They are then required to complete a period of supervision, often a less intense version of probation, and participate in other programs such as drug and alcohol counseling and community service. After successful completion of the program, individuals can have their charges dismissed and later expunged from their criminal record. Amanda did not have to report in person to her probation officer and was not subject to random drug screenings. This program had an online system, which she would log in to once a week to report that she was doing okay and following the rules.

At first, Amanda was not aware of how the ARD probation program worked, so she was on her best behavior when she was first charged. My parents told me they saw a lot of positive changes in Amanda right after her charges went through and her probation period was officially active. My mom and step-dad told me she was "coming around more, doing a lot better, and spending time with them." She was even hanging out at the house and watching TV with Keith, my stepdad, whom she'd never really gotten along with because he always called her out when she was obviously high and trying to hide it. He told me how impressed he was with her and how normal she seemed during this time.

Amanda made it clear that the fear of going to jail was enough motivation for her to get her act together. Before she learned how the ARD program worked, she was prepared to pass her drug tests and report to her probation officer as required. However, after a month or two, she learned that she would not even have to take drug tests or report to her probation officer in person. Before we knew it, she was back to her old ways. She rarely came around my parents, barely talked to me, and was once again back to using IV drugs.

Over the next year, 2017, I barely talked to Amanda. I wanted to keep my distance because I knew she wasn't doing well. I knew if she was doing better, I would hear from her more. But the only news I ever heard was from my parents, and it was always bad. She would often show up to my mom's house high on heroin and meth but would deny being on any drugs. My parents would send me videos of Amanda while she was high and struggling to form sentences. A video that will always stand out in my mind is from July 4, 2017—I remember it well because of the holiday. It was by far the worst I had ever seen my sister.

I opened the video message from my mom and sat in shock, watching my sister. She had shown up to my mom's house clearly fucked up. She could barely stand up straight or form a coherent sentence. It's hard to describe what this looked like. She was saying things someone might say if they were half asleep—just starting to fall asleep and half dreaming, but trying to stay awake at the same time. You may have had this happen: you wake up and catch yourself saying something totally ridiculous and then realize it's probably time to go to bed. That's exactly what this was like, but worse because she wasn't just sleepy. She was completely disheveled. Her skin was picked apart, her eyes were barely open, and she kept whipping her head back and forth like her neck was about to break.

She stood in the kitchen with her eyes shut as she attempted to converse with my parents. Her hair was pulled back in a messy bun and looked like it hadn't been washed in weeks. My parents were filming her and she didn't even notice, because her eyes were always either closed or rolling back in her head. She rocked back and forth and held on to the table as she tried to maintain her balance. Between her grunts and moans, she cried out, "MOM! Are you getting me that or what?" She was antsy as she waited for my mom to give her something, but my mom was in shock, watching her.

My stepdad finally asked, "What are you on, Amanda?"

She responded loudly: "I AM NOT ON ANYTHING, KEITH. I AM JUST VERY, VERY HOT, OKAY?"

"But you can barely stand. Your eyes are barely open."

"WHAT? I am not on anything. Oh. MY. GOD."

"Why are you denying it?"

"I am not on anything, I barely slept last night."

"Oh, come on, that's always the excuse."

Amanda started shouting: "I BROKE UP WITH SHANNON. I AM VERY STRESSED OUT. SOME CRACKHEAD BITCH BEAT THE SHIT OUT OF ME LAST NIGHT. I AM NOT ON DRUGS. I AM JUST VERY STRESSED OUT."

"That doesn't look stressed out to me. Stressed out doesn't look like you do right now."

"Listen, Keith, I'm not going to stand here and argue with you. I'm not on fucking drugs, okay?"

"Well, it sure doesn't look like it."

"Whatever. That's your opinion. OH MY FUCKING GOD." Amanda slammed her fist down on the counter angrily.

The video ended shortly after Amanda started yelling and continually denying being on drugs. Up until this point, Amanda had somehow convinced my mom that she was sober, mostly. But as time went on, it became harder and harder for Amanda to deny her drug use. Later that day, I received another video from my mom.

The second video was shot at my sister's apartment. My mom filmed Amanda as she sat at her kitchen table. Amanda wore only a bra and again kept swinging her head up and down as she mumbled words that didn't make sense. She was starting to nod off, but was still awake enough to carry on these pseudo-interactions. Nothing she said made any sense.

Watching these videos forced something in me I can't really explain; I had just had enough. I couldn't see her act this way anymore, and I couldn't stand seeing my parents go through this over and over again. I knew my sister was still on probation and the only thing that truly scared her enough to change was the fear of going to jail. But what was the point of even being on probation if she was doing the exact same shit that got her on probation in the first place? Not to mention, her apartment had become "the place" where many other drug users would hang out. Half of them would crash there because they were couch surfing and didn't have a real place to stay. Amanda was the queen of codependent relationships and always wanted to be "the savior" to her friends. But she was never going to get any better or get away from that lifestyle if she wasn't held accountable for her actions. I knew I had to find a way to get in touch with her probation officer.

The hard part was that I had no idea who her probation officer was, how to get in touch with them, or how to report her. My sister certainly was not going to offer this information up to me if I asked her, so I had to figure out a way to find out without her knowing. Fortunately, I remembered that Ian, one of my close friends who still lived in our hometown, happened to be a former probation officer. I reached out to him, hoping that he might be able to connect me with someone who could help.

The next day, Ian got back to me and said he had spoken with the head of the county's probation office. They were going to address my sister's situation right away. I felt an immediate rush of relief, like a shot of adrenaline, throughout my entire body. *Finally,* she was going to be held accountable for her actions. A part of me also felt guilty, though. I knew how pissed off Amanda was going to be at me, my mom, and my entire family. It's hard to explain this feeling: knowing deep down that you did the right thing, yet having this overwhelming feeling of "oh shit, things are about to get real."

It didn't take more than a few days until Amanda started flipping out and asking around about who called her probation officer on her. Apparently, she had heard from her probation officer and needed to report for a check-in. I held steadfast in my knowledge that I did the right thing. No matter how much she carried on, I had no plans to tell her it was me. I felt bad for my mom because Amanda assumed she was the one who called. I had managed to pull the strings "behind the scenes," and because I wasn't talking to my sister much, she didn't suspect me. I told my mom to deny it was her. She wasn't lying, and she had no reason to feel guilty. It was my doing, and I knew I had done the right thing in the long run.

I planned on never saying anything to Amanda under the current circumstances. I told myself that if she was clean in a year or so and in a much better place, maybe I would tell her. At times, it was difficult for me to keep this secret because

Amanda was being so hard on my mom, saying hurtful things to make her feel guilty. But realistically, I knew that the situation would pass and that it didn't matter if Amanda knew who had told on her. The important part was that she was *finally* starting to be held accountable for her actions, at least in theory, because probation would be checking in on her more regularly. But I quickly learned probation isn't that simple. One failed drug test doesn't equal immediate jail time. She was going to be given a lot of chances, but at least someone was finally keeping tabs on her.

CHAPTER 7

FINALLY, A NEW ROCK BOTTOM

After her overdose in 2016, Amanda lost custody of her son, Christopher, who she always said was her "only reason to live." She didn't get along with Christopher's father, whom she had separated from when Christopher was only two years old. Now if she wanted to even have a conversation with Christopher, his father dictated if and when she would be allowed to. I wish this situation had motivated Amanda to do better, try harder, and get herself back together. Unfortunately, the guilt of losing Christopher made things worse, and she only fell further and further into her addiction. And even though probation was now involved, she took a long time to find even a sliver of motivation to get sober again.

During this time, I tried my best to practice detachment and live my life without constantly worrying about Amanda. Thankfully, being in Nashville and away from my family made this a bit easier. On August 4, 2017, Cort and I got engaged at our home, surrounded by our closest friends. It was truly one of the happiest days of my life, free from any stress or family-related drama. It was just me, Cort, and the new family of friends we had made in Nashville.

I soaked up the excitement and bliss of our engagement the best I could during those first few weeks. I knew it was only a matter of time before I had to start wedding planning and making big decisions about our special day. This was stressful because while we were in the process of planning our wedding, Amanda was still actively using IV drugs. Growing up, I had always imagined my sister being my maid of honor, but I was in a tough spot. It was challenging for me to even picture Amanda staying alive until our wedding the following September. And, of course, I had major trust issues when it came to her. So I eventually decided not to include her in my bridal party and felt that an invitation to the wedding would be more than reasonable given the point she was at in her life.

I know this sounds harsh, but our relationship was strained, and I wasn't going to risk my mental health for the sake of pleasing my family. This bothered Amanda, but I had to be honest with her. We had a difficult conversation over the phone that ended in a screaming match. I said, "Until you are clean and sober, I can't trust you to be in my wedding. I'm sorry." Of course, she took offense to this and found a way to turn her guilt and anger around on me. She said things like, "You just think you're better than me," and "You don't know the meaning of family." I had to learn to brush these comments off. I knew that if Amanda were sober one day, she would understand why I couldn't have her in my wedding. I didn't hold on to hope that this would happen, though. At this point, I had given up on her ever being sober or living a somewhat normal life again.

After I reported Amanda to probation in July 2017, she began having to report to her probation officer in person on a weekly basis. The accountability that came with having to report did eventually help, but it took a long time. For months, she failed drug test after drug test. Surprisingly, and disappointingly, this didn't result in any consequences, so naturally she kept on using. She needed to hit her "new rock bottom" on her own terms before she could realize that there was no way out of the life she was living.

By early fall in 2017, Amanda's addiction had spiraled to a new level. Based on what she told me several years later, at the time all she did was use drugs, sleep, and occasionally go to work when she still had a job. Over the course of a few months, she lost about fifty pounds. I'll always remember the first picture she sent me after she had lost all of that weight. She had changed significantly over the course of a few months. She now weighed less than me and started asking me to give her clothing I no longer wanted. Before this, Amanda had worn a size extra-large in tops and fourteen in jeans. She was now asking me for size small tops and size six jeans. And this was in the span of a few months with no exercise involved whatsoever. She had simply wasted away due to excessive drug use and not eating. It was the type of weight loss journey no one would be excited about.

In October 2017, Amanda started talking about going back to rehab. She and Shannon had hit their necessary rock bottom. Their relationship was toxic, and they both knew it. Amanda claimed, "I just need to get away from it all." And she knew the only way to gain our family's support was to leave Shannon behind and go back to rehab. That month, she finally agreed to go back to a twenty-eight-day inpatient program.

This was her third inpatient stay since 2014. After her last rehab stay, in July 2016, she had relapsed almost immediately and later failed out of outpatient drug counseling as a result of her drug use and noncompliance with the program. Amanda never seemed to take outpatient counseling seriously and always managed to get kicked out of those programs after a few months due to either poor attendance or failing multiple drug screens. Of course, she would never own up to these things as they were happening. As I mentioned before, we would always find out months later. Willingly agreeing and initiating the steps to go back to an inpatient program was huge for Amanda. She needed to commit for a month's time, would not have access to her phone, and would not be able to use no matter how bad her cravings were. This was the ultimate surrender.

While this was a huge step, there were also a ton of concerns regarding follow-up care after discharge. After her first two times in rehab, Amanda came home and relapsed right away. I learned through my experience with Nar-Anon that the initial twenty-eight days are very important for getting clean and detoxing, but they are the very first baby steps to the entire process. Basically, the person with addiction gets out of rehab just when they're starting to get their feet wet. They have no idea what they're really doing yet and haven't even begun to experience life sober. This was my biggest concern for Amanda. I worried that she would resist going to sober living in either a halfway or recovery house following her discharge. However, this time around, my family had learned from our previous mistakes and my dad was ready to terminate her lease at any moment. We were prepared to give her no other options: either go to sober living or you don't have a place to live.

My family and I obviously hoped this time in rehab would be different, but we also didn't want to get our hopes up. As Amanda prepared to go back to rehab, we were all aboard the "Help Amanda at All Costs Train," yet again. We had to send her off with money and plenty of cigarettes and make sure she had everything she needed throughout her stay. We kept in touch via phone calls and letters and supported her however we could.

While supportive, I was also somewhat cynical during Amanda's time at rehab. It's hard as a family member to continue to root for someone over and over again when all they do is constantly disappoint you. Sure, I wanted to believe she would get better this time, but *trusting* in that was a whole other issue. Amanda had betrayed my trust a long time ago. The first time was when she first used heroin, and the second time was when she relapsed the same day she was discharged home from rehab. What's that saying? "Fool me once, shame on you; fool me twice, shame on me." I was *so* over letting Amanda fool me into believing she was serious about recovery. This was now her third time in rehab, and I had very little faith that she would actually take things seriously.

Amanda's willingness and desire to go to a sober living community after inpatient rehab would be a good indicator of how serious she was about recovery. Her follow-through with getting a sponsor, going to meetings, and becoming part of a recovery community would also be very telling. I kept my expectations low; it was hard to remain positive when she had never seemed to take recovery seriously in the past. However, during her last week in rehab, Amanda, surprisingly, called to give me an update on her discharge plans. She sounded really good over the phone—optimistic and excited about her future. She told me she planned to go to a recovery house after discharge and finally understood she couldn't go back to her apartment, or even the town where my family lived, if she wanted to remain serious about recovery. I was honestly shocked. This was a huge step for her and the most commitment she had ever shown related to her recovery. My dad moved quickly to terminate the lease at her apartment and moved all her stuff into storage. Amanda now had nowhere else to go but to a recovery house, and we gave her no other options.

Amanda was discharged from rehab on November 22, 2017, and transitioned directly to a recovery house, where she planned to live indefinitely. My Aunt Anne Marie, who is an angel on this Earth, became Amanda's emergency contact and primary support person as she entered recovery. My mom and Amanda always butted heads, and my dad was just over it after living with and supporting her financially for many years. So by default and because she cared so deeply for Amanda, my aunt took on this role and did everything she could to help her. This included driving more than an hour to take her to doctor's appointments, pick up groceries, and take her to meetings with her attorney for child custody matters. She was always there for Amanda. I know that, deep down, Amanda appreciated her; I can feel Amanda telling me that in my bones as I write this, but at the time, she definitely didn't know how to fully express gratitude like a normal human being.

Amanda's brain after getting out of rehab was *wild*. The first time she called me after discharge, I was completely caught off guard by what I heard on the other end of the phone. I guess I expected her to sound normal—you know, like anyone else who's sober—and be calm and rational in the things she was saying. However, I couldn't have been more mistaken, and if she hadn't been in a recovery house, I may have thought she was under the influence of something. She sounded manic; and I mean *manic*. She was talking so unbelievably fast that I could barely understand her. She was going on about things that didn't make sense and weren't connected. Her thoughts were all over the place. She was also short of breath, as she was walking up and down the street, going in and out of a gas station because she kept forgetting things she needed to buy. When I tried asking what she was talking about and expressed concern about her behavior, she got upset with me. She was easily frustrated in early recovery, and me questioning her only made things worse.

Amanda's mental state went back and forth like this for a while at the beginning of her recovery, and sometimes later into her recovery, too. I learned that her brain chemistry had changed dramatically due to years of excessive drug use and she was still learning how to cope with normal everyday stressors. According to the NIDA, brain imaging of individuals in early recovery shows less activity in the prefrontal cortex. This area of the brain is associated with judgment, decision-making, and moderating social behavior, so it makes sense that Amanda would often call me panicked and overwhelmed in early recovery. She was still learning how to function as a normal adult in society, and her brain wasn't up to speed.

Whenever any minor stressful event occurred, Amanda would call me in a full panic, asking for help or asking what she should do. She didn't know how to respond to or cope with any stressors that came her way. She essentially had the coping skills of a young teenager, the age she was when she first started using drugs. I was now the "older sister." She was learning a lot of these skills all over again, and the longer she stayed sober, the easier it would be for her brain to start adapting to and coping with everyday stressors.

It was challenging for me to deal with and understand what she was going through at the time. Don't get me wrong; I was happy for Amanda. She was finally living in a recovery house and taking action steps towards a better life. I was by no means judging her; I was just very concerned about her mental well-being and how she was going to be able to handle stress and this new life she was living, *on her own*, in a new city and away from my family. I had to learn the hard way that even though Amanda was *sober*, her brain and coping skills had a lot of catching up to do.

Despite these early struggles, Amanda remained committed and settled into her first recovery house relatively quickly. Recovery houses are a great transition for those in early recovery because they provide structure and community—and require residents to follow certain "house rules" in order to stay there. Amanda was forced to go to ninety meetings in ninety days, which helped her get closer to her roommates, who were all there doing the same thing, and to seek out a sponsor for the very first time. The meetings were required to be twelve-step meetings, and Amanda chose a Narcotics Anonymous (NA) program. She was also required to get a job within the first few weeks of living at the recovery house.

Amanda found her first job at a local pizza shop and was finally starting to make some of her own money for the first time in a while. However, even though she had a job, we had to help her pay rent until she could get on her feet. This stressed me out and annoyed me at times, especially because Amanda had no sense of money management. She was earning on her own now but would often waste paychecks on unnecessary things like office supplies or perfume. She had no idea how to prioritize her spending or how to save money for things she actually needed, like food. She also smoked a pack a day and had no intention of slowing down. I had to remind myself that even though her money management skills still needed a lot of work, *she was trying*. And I would continue to help her as long as she remained committed.

For several months, Amanda made steady progress in her recovery. She was on a treatment regimen that included a monthly shot of Vivitrol, an opioid antagonist drug that blocks opioid cravings. Vivitrol binds to and blocks the opioid receptors throughout the body, so not only does it reduce cravings, but it also blocks the ability to get high on opioids. This protocol was working well for Amanda because she didn't have to worry about taking a pill every day, as she would if she were on Suboxone or methadone, and the recovery house staff held her accountable for getting the shot on time every month so it stayed active in her system.

Amanda continued to work at her job at the pizza place, and eventually started paying some of her rent. She regularly attended meetings with her roommates and found a sponsor she liked. She even started posting and sharing parts of her recovery journey on her Facebook page. This was surprising to see because she had never wanted to publicly share her issues with substance abuse. I was proud of her for sharing her story and knew that this could potentially help others seek out help as well.

In just a few months' time, Amanda had made significant progress and demonstrated more responsibility than she had in years. I felt hopeful that she would continue down this path and maybe one day even work in recovery herself. She talked about that as a dream of hers. She would always say to me, "I don't want to use drugs, Nicole. I don't want to live that life anymore." And I really did believe her. But part of me also worried that life might catch up to her. She still struggled with managing stress and handling the mundane things of everyday life. She often made simple situations complicated and lacked self-awareness to the point of being unable to take responsibility for her actions. For example, my dad had paid for her monthly bus pass, but she would continually run late and miss the bus. She would then call me and insist that I order her an Uber that very minute, not caring about what I was doing. I had to drop everything and immediately order her the Uber, or she would get angry with me. It didn't matter if I was working or driving; she would act like the world was going to end if I didn't drop everything I was doing to help her. This was getting old really quick.

Amanda was selfish and never felt bad about asking for too much. I was paying her rent about half the time, and she was still asking me for money on top of that. I was starting to feel like I was being taken advantage of. I wanted to help her, but not if it was preventing her from being responsible for herself and learning how to manage her affairs as a "recovered" adult. As the months dragged on, I grew tired of constantly giving and started asking her tough questions that she never wanted to answer. I would ask her where she was spending all her money and why she was constantly broke. I would challenge her on why she couldn't ask her roommates for rides and how many meetings she was attending after she had finished her ninety meetings in ninety days. I was getting tired of the constant lack of appreciation. But Amanda hated being questioned and started lashing out whenever I pushed her too far.

Eventually, she got tired of me hounding her and started talking to me less. By the beginning of the new year in 2018, Amanda's behaviors had started spiraling out of control, and I was starting to worry that she wasn't doing as well as she wanted us to believe. She stopped calling, and when we did talk, she seemed irritated about all sorts of things and would often hang up in a hurry. She didn't want to answer any questions related to her recovery, like how meetings were going or how she was working the steps with her sponsor. I wish I could say my parents and family picked up on these same red flags that I always did, but that wasn't the case. Not long after she started acting this way, in February 2018, Amanda was actually *kicked out* of her recovery house.

We learned that Shannon, Amanda's ex-girlfriend, had come down to the same city where Amanda was living to start her own recovery journey. Despite being at different recovery houses, they ran into each other at a few meetings, and soon after, they started spending time together again. Kathy, the woman in charge of the recovery house, did not want Amanda spending time with Shannon, as she knew it would jeopardize Amanda's recovery. Amanda was warned several times about hanging out with Shannon and was given multiple chances. Of course, she was her stubborn self and didn't listen. Eventually her behaviors, on top of her misuse one of her prescriptions—which I didn't learn about until much later—got her kicked out of her very first recovery house.

Amanda called me the night this happened to explain her side of the story. She was surprisingly calm—she must have practiced what she wanted to say before she called. She recounted what had happened between her and Kathy, and said she was accused of spending more time with Shannon than she actually was. She swore up and down that she was still sober, going to meetings, and actively participating in her recovery. I wanted to believe her, and for some reason, I did this time. She begged me to help her get into a hotel until she could find somewhere else to live. I obliged but told her if she was lying to me, I was absolutely done with her and wouldn't be helping her out any longer. She promised that she wasn't lying and gave me the information for a local hotel, where I put her up for a few days until we found her somewhere else to live.

A few days later, I helped Amanda pay the security deposit and two weeks' rent for a new house, where she would rent a room on a weekly basis until she had a longer-term plan. I had no idea where she was staying as I was not familiar with the city where she lived. All I knew was that she would have several housemates and wouldn't have the same rules or restrictions as she would at a traditional recovery house. She promised she was still going to meetings and wasn't using drugs, so I decided to trust her despite my better judgment and the warning signs I described earlier. Unfortunately, it didn't take long for Amanda to confirm my suspicions.

CHAPTER 8

TOUGH LOVE

Loving someone with addiction has many ups and downs. Often, just when you think you're in a good place, the rug is pulled out from underneath you, and you realize they have taken two steps forward but three steps back at the same time. That's how I started to feel about Amanda in the early stages of her recovery from late 2017 into early 2018. Sometimes she would surprise me and talk to me with clarity and composure, which is why I chose to believe her after she got kicked out of her recovery house. However, at other times she was completely unhinged. From day to day, I never knew which side of her I was going to get. But I understood the importance of her keeping in touch with me. I had learned by this point that if she wasn't talking to me, then she was up to no good, and I had to remind myself of this even when she was pissing me off and asking me for rent money or to order her Ubers all over town. As long as she was talking to me, that usually meant she was okay, even if she was still a work in progress.

However, after I helped Amanda find a new place to live in February 2018, it didn't take long before things started to change. She started calling less, and when she did call, she always needed something. She had lost her job at the pizza place, and it was taking her a while to find a new one, although I wasn't sure how much effort she was putting into the search. It was exhausting dealing with and worrying about her all the time. It was starting to become clear that she was not working her program and had fallen off the wagon. I couldn't ignore the warning signs any longer. Amanda never wanted to admit this to me when I asked her, so I stopped asking. I knew what she was up to and didn't need her to admit to relapsing to confirm that's what was going on. She continued to tell my family she was sober, even though her behavior had drastically changed and she barely called to check in with anyone at this point.

Though she would not admit it at the time, we later learned that she had relapsed on "bath salts," which apparently were marketed around where she lived as "ecstasy." It didn't matter what she was taking, though; once she had one drug back in her system, it triggered cravings for her drug of choice: heroin. A day or two after taking bath salts, she started using heroin again, and the rest is history. Communication dwindled, meetings stopped, and recovery halted.

We eventually learned that Shannon was with Amanda while she relapsed and had brought the bath salts to Amanda's house, where they did them together. I can't say this caused her to relapse, though, because as I now understand, Amanda's choices were 100 percent her own. She knew hanging out with Shannon could cause her to relapse. She had learned in her multiple rehab stays and NA meetings that *people*, *places*, and *things* highly affect her choices, behaviors, and ability to stay clean and sober. She knew being around Shannon would bring back memories and emotions involved with drug use and put her in a more vulnerable position to relapse. However, she didn't want to admit this to herself, and she most certainly didn't want to admit it to us.

Before *officially* learning that she had relapsed in late March 2018, I had grown tired of paying Amanda's rent, as she only called me when she needed something. I told myself I would only support her financially if I knew she was putting the work into her recovery, but at this point, it was obvious to me that she was not. She still hadn't found a job and wasn't going to meetings. Every day I wondered to myself what she could be doing with all her time. She eventually moved on to asking other members of my family to pay her rent and somehow managed to find the money to stay in that house for a little over a month. However, in true Amanda fashion, she couldn't stay away from drama and was eventually involved in an altercation with one of her roommates that led to her being kicked out of the house. She again needed to find somewhere else to live, and because she didn't have a job or financial resources, she would need help figuring that out.

Amanda knew I wasn't going to give her money until she was clean again, so she didn't even try to call me and ask for help. Instead, she called my mom and somehow convinced her she was still sober and just needed a place to stay for a few days. To this day, I don't know how she explained getting kicked out of the house, but somehow she was able to convince my mom to put her up in a hotel for three nights. She carried all of her stuff, in garbage bags and storage bins, to the hotel and stayed there with Shannon for three days. No one heard from her for those three days, and I had a horrible feeling this wasn't going to end well for her.

On the day Amanda was supposed to check out of the hotel, I suspected we might hear from her, either begging for money for additional nights or asking for help renting another room somewhere nearby. Checkout was at 11:00 a.m., and what do you know? At 10:50, Amanda started calling me and anyone in the family who would possibly give her money. I knew what was going on and what she had been doing while she was there: nothing except using heroin for three straight days. I knew this pattern would only continue if we enabled her and gave her money. After she called me, I called and texted everyone in my family and encouraged them not to give her money. My mom already felt terrible for putting her up in the hotel when she didn't realize Amanda had been using. I wasn't going to allow that to happen again.

I quickly made the rounds and covered everyone who I knew she might call, to prevent them from giving her money to stay in the hotel for another night. I told everyone she had relapsed and we needed to cut her off unless she agreed to go back to rehab. When Amanda worked her way back to me, I answered the phone and warned her that we all knew what she was up to and that if she continued this behavior, she was going to lose all of us. I told her we would help her, but only if she agreed to go back to rehab. I said, "You've come too far to go back to this again. I'm not mad at you, but I will not enable you to destroy your life. If you agree to go to rehab, Anne Marie will come get you right now and help you find a bed somewhere. But we will not take Shannon with you, and we will not give you any more money if you stay with her." Amanda absolutely refused to leave Shannon or go back to rehab. She said, "I would rather stay on the street than go back to rehab again."

Keep in mind that it was the middle of March in Pennsylvania and still quite cold; staying on the street would not be ideal. But she had made her decision, and I wasn't going to beg her to change her mind. She knew where we stood.

Amanda called me several times later that day, begging me to change my mind and reconsider giving her money for a hotel. She tried every trick to manipulate me, my mom, and my aunt and convince us that we were horrible family members because of our decision to cut her off. But I had never felt surer of anything in my entire life. We *needed* to do this *for her*. If we didn't, she would continue to repeat the same behaviors she had been exhibiting for weeks. My mom was hesitant and hated the idea of Amanda being on the street overnight with all of her belongings and nowhere to go. Of course, I wasn't thrilled about it either, but Amanda had been catered to for her entire life. Regardless of whether or not she had a job, was using, or was communicating with my parents, my dad had always made sure she had a roof over her head until she went to rehab this last time.

I knew the only way for Amanda to change was for her to clearly see that her actions had consequences. None of us had put those bath salts into her system. None of us had called Shannon to trigger her old drug habits. And none of us had shot the heroin into Amanda's body. She had done all of those things *on her own*. It was time for her to own up to her actions and experience a new rock bottom. We weren't bailing her out this time.

Despite her dozen or so attempts to guilt me and my family into changing our minds, including a late-night call around eleven o'clock from out on a street corner, we stood firm: we weren't giving her any money. Amanda spent her first night on the street in the cold March weather. I couldn't help but feel horrible for what I had done; the guilt involved with this shit was mind-boggling. At the same time, I knew we had done the right thing and kept reminding myself and my mom that this was *Amanda's choice*. We offered to help if she agreed to go back to rehab and leave Shannon. *Amanda* chose to stay on the streets and stay with Shannon. We chose *not to enable her*.

I tossed and turned all night worrying about Amanda. It was so cold that night; I couldn't imagine being out on the street in those frigid temperatures. I also couldn't even begin to process what might be going on in Amanda's head. How far gone was she that she would choose to stay out in the cold rather than accept help and go back to rehab? I really thought this approach would work, but she chose to be *homeless* rather than give up her addiction. A million thoughts ran through my head as I worried about her. *What if she doesn't make it through the night? Where will she sleep? What if she experiences hypothermia? What if her phone dies and she has no way to reach us if she changes her mind?* It was hard to make my monkey mind stop. I guess it eventually did because somehow, I fell asleep and woke up the next morning with several messages from Amanda.

Her first text came just after midnight and said, "One of Shannon's friends just picked us up and took us to her place. Call me tomorrow, we need to talk." The next text said, "Nicole, please call me when you wake up. I will go back to rehab."

All I could think was, *Wow, it worked.* Apparently, Amanda had received the message. I was so happy to hear they didn't have to spend the night freezing out on the street. I wouldn't wish that on anyone. But I knew Amanda needed this experience to understand that her family was not going to bail her out of every bad situation just because she begged or manipulated us into doing so. I needed her to know we were not going to enable her because that was going to do more harm than good. She needed to see that she was accountable for her actions and wouldn't always be protected from the harsh realities of her choices.

I called Amanda, and we came up with a plan for her to go back to rehab. I arranged for my Aunt Anne Marie to pick Amanda up and bring her back home to stay with someone in the family for a few days until we found her a bed. Amanda told me she had lost most of her belongings, including an expensive laptop, during her time on the street. She said she had asked some homeless people to watch her stuff while she went into a pizza place to get something to eat and charge her cell phone. When she came back out, both the homeless people and her stuff were gone.

I didn't know what to believe, but I didn't feel any remorse about Amanda losing her stuff. I wish I could say my mom shared the same sentiment. To this day, my mom still gets upset about how Amanda lost her laptop and a ton of other belongings because we made her stay out on the street. Of course, I hated that my mom was upset, but I knew deep down this wasn't our fault. This experience, although hard, was an important part of Amanda's recovery journey. Luckily, this time Amanda understood that we meant business.

CHAPTER 9

LONGEST STRETCH OF SOBRIETY

After Amanda agreed to go back to rehab, my aunt drove almost two hours to pick her up and take her for a drug and alcohol evaluation. If you remember, this is the first step when pursuing inpatient placement, as we learned after Amanda's first overdose in 2014. Amanda was surprisingly agreeable to this despite her earlier resistance. I'm not sure if something happened between her and Shannon or if she just accepted that we would all cut her off if she didn't get her shit together, but for whatever reason, she was fully ready to get right back into rehab. This felt like a miracle compared to where we had been with her just a few days prior. Addiction was full of surprises, sometimes good, but often bad, so I was thankful this was working out. I was also grateful to have my aunt's help with this process.

From this point forward, my Aunt Anne Marie and I started handling the majority of Amanda's affairs. Amanda didn't like to fully involve my mom because she asked a lot of questions and they always butted heads. As I said before, my dad backed off quite a bit after Amanda started using heroin. He couldn't handle the stress, and distancing himself became his coping mechanism. So it was up to me and my aunt, and we took on the responsibility of getting Amanda into a new rehab facility and communicating with staff and others involved in her care.

At the drug and alcohol evaluation, the evaluators recommended inpatient rehab and started the process of finding Amanda a bed. After being through this several times, Amanda started to become more selective about which rehab facility she would agree to go to. She never wanted to go back to somewhere she had already been. I'm not sure if going back would feel like admitting she had relapsed, or what her thinking was, but she would only agree to go to certain places. After a few hours, they found a rehab that Amanda agreed to. In March 2018, she entered her fourth rehab facility in as many years.

Amanda needed to sort through her things and find out exactly what she needed to take with her; she had lost a lot of her belongings during her partial night on the street. My aunt took Amanda to my mom's house for a few days to get her stuff together while they waited for a bed to open at her chosen rehab. Unfortunately, this didn't work out for very long. The next day, Amanda called me, upset and claiming that my mom was "holding her hostage" and treating her "like a child." Amanda had asked if she could leave my mom's house to go meet up with some friends, and my mom told her no. As mentioned, Amanda hated being told what to do and became extremely upset. I tried my best to de-escalate the situation, but I couldn't blame my mom for saying no. Amanda was only two days removed from living out on the streets and injecting heroin into her body multiple times a day. How could my mom live with herself if she let Amanda go and something happened while she was waiting to get into a new rehab? Amanda hadn't necessarily earned any privileges after everything she had put us through up to this point.

Amanda eventually called my aunt and begged her to pick her up from my mom's house. My aunt said Amanda could stay with her for a few days until she was admitted to rehab. My aunt also lived with our eighty-six-year-old grandmother with dementia, so she had a lot on her plate already. They gave it a shot, but after only one day, my aunt decided it was too much and paid for Amanda to stay in a hotel for a few days while they waited for Amanda's bed to be ready.

Since this was Amanda's fourth time in rehab, we knew the drill and prepared accordingly. We again spent money on all the "essentials": cigarettes, toiletries, and makeup (she had lost all of hers when her belongings were stolen on the street). Having to support her both emotionally and financially every time she relapsed was a lot of work. But at least in rehab, we would know she was safe and not at risk of overdosing at any given moment.

During this time, dealing with Amanda took an unbelievable amount of patience because she was still in the limbo stage between being high and sober. She never wanted to enter rehab sober, which is probably why she didn't want to stay with my mom or aunt while she waited for her bed. She always said to me, "Nicole, no addict is going to go to rehab sober. It just doesn't work that way." So I assumed she would be using up until the day she was admitted. And I was right; every time she went into rehab, she went through a detox program first and then transitioned to the traditional women's unit. I now understand that she was continuing her drug use until she was admitted to avoid being dope sick. In rehab, the detox programs help with the withdrawal symptoms while also providing MAT to avoid dope sickness and cravings altogether.

This time was no different. Amanda was admitted for opioid detox before transitioning to the women's unit. After settling into treatment, though, her overall attitude during this rehab stay was drastically different than during previous ones. She communicated with me frequently and was honest and open about her past. She shared stories with me that I thought she would never even verbalize within earshot of me. She told me about her relapse and how she had used bath salts, thinking they were ecstasy. During one of our first phone calls, she said, "Shannon came over and was all excited about trying ecstasy. It wasn't our drug of choice, so we thought we could have some fun and it would be a one-time thing. But I don't know how to explain it, Nicole. Well, first of all, she didn't have ecstasy. It was bath salts, and it was absolutely awful. Afterwards, I felt so bad all I wanted was heroin. And I just didn't care anymore. We shot up the next day. And then continued every day after that."

These conversations were difficult to have, but I was happy, and I was proud of Amanda for being honest with me. I appreciated this small peek into her life—it was eye-opening to say the least. Previously, she had kept the details from me and wouldn't open up about her life and her experience with addiction. It was interesting to see behind the curtain, and this helped me gain a better perspective of what really went on inside her mind. I was also proud of her for jumping right back into treatment, even if we had to cut her off financially to persuade her to get there.

Amanda and I talked every other day while she was in treatment. She alternated between calling my mom or aunt and calling me during her two daily calls. I appreciated her keeping me in the loop—this was more than we had communicated during any of her previous rehab stays. We discussed discharge plans closer to the end of treatment, and I helped her research several recovery houses within the general area of the rehab facility. She didn't have her apartment anymore and couldn't come back home afterwards, so at least we had peace of mind, knowing she had no other options besides continuing treatment in a recovery house.

After four weeks in inpatient rehab, on April 23, 2018, Amanda was discharged and transitioned immediately to a new recovery house in Lemoyne, a small borough just outside of Harrisburg, Pennsylvania. The house was located in a quiet neighborhood, but close enough to the main street that she could walk to potential job opportunities. She seemed to like it there and fit in well with her housemates. She was required to find a job right away and work at least twenty hours per week. She needed to continue aftercare treatment, which for her would be some sort of outpatient counseling, and attend four AA or NA meetings per week. She also had a nightly curfew of ten o'clock during the week and midnight on weekends.

Amanda started intensive outpatient drug counseling right away and attended regular NA meetings with her housemates. Within the first few weeks of starting NA, she found a sponsor whom she raved about. She said this sponsor was going to "push her" more than she had ever been pushed, and she was excited for that challenge. She would frequently say to me, "I don't want to do drugs, Nicole. I have no desire to live that life anymore. I'm going to do this for myself and for my son."

Christopher was still living with his dad, who had full custody at this point. Amanda had to go through the court system to gain any parental rights back after losing custody. Soon after transitioning to the new recovery house in April 2018, she started working with a court-appointed attorney who, throughout the next year, helped her gain back some parental rights and supervised visitation with her son. This process wasn't easy, but it was one of Amanda's greatest motivators in her recovery process.

Amanda eventually found a job at a grocery store and started paying her own rent most of the time. I wish I could say she was able to fully support herself in all other areas too, but financial management was challenging for her. For years—controlled by her opioid addiction—Amanda spent all of her money on drugs. Her paycheck would be gone within hours or days, and all of it was spent either directly on drugs or to pay back people she had borrowed money from to buy drugs. So while having a regular paycheck was a big step in the right direction for her, managing her finances did not come easy.

I used to get so angry with Amanda because she would blow the last fifty to one hundred dollars she had left from her check on nonsense at a convenience store or on pricey lunches for herself during work and then expect me to bail her out by giving her spending money until she got her next paycheck. It was hard for me to trust her, let alone give her money to spend on whatever the hell she pleased. But I was becoming a regular at the Western Union desk inside our local Kroger store because I had to send her money almost every week. It was frustrating, but I tried to remind myself that as long as she was working a program, going to meetings, and communicating with me regularly, I would support her. Who else did she have?

The truth is that being a family member of a person with opioid addiction is not easy. There is constant worry. There is constant nagging. There is constant fear. Fear of relapse, fear of her losing her job, fear of the next phone call. There is a constant presence of fear that never goes away. All of this fear was hard to ignore, despite the fact that she was actually doing pretty well for a change. Amanda's time in this recovery house ended up being her longest stretch of sobriety. Looking back on it now, I can recognize just how much progress she made. But at the time, it was difficult to see the progress because it was always clouded by *mess*.

Mess is how I would describe Amanda's life, especially in early recovery, when she would first come out of treatment and transition to a recovery house. She would often call me out of the blue, flipping out about something totally random. She wouldn't give me any background details or any warning whatsoever, but she would expect me to drop whatever I was doing and come to her aid right then and there. I could have been at work, at an appointment, in the middle of dinner; it didn't matter, because the world revolved around her. And this is how it felt for a long time.

Looking back now, I can see how far she had come, and I know she was reaching out to me because I had told her to. At the time, though, it was a lot to handle. I wasn't used to that level of intensity or drama in my life. I am a calm person, and I like to keep things that way. I don't typically go from extreme highs to extreme lows, and none of my friends do either, so dealing with this level of drama on a regular basis took me out of my comfort zone. But I did it. No matter how annoyed, frustrated, or worked up Amanda made me, I always answered her calls. I always helped her out. *Because she was sober and that was all that mattered.*

This was the strategy I stuck with as long as I knew Amanda was clean and sober. Unlike other members of my family, I trusted my gut and always knew when something was off with her.

Amanda had her longest stretch of sobriety in 2018, about nine to ten months in total. She became actively involved in the recovery community, regularly attended NA meetings, worked with a sponsor, and even volunteered at recovery-related events. She held down her job at the grocery store and, despite struggling to manage her finances, she eventually paid her own rent completely on her own at the recovery house. She also traveled with my family to Nashville to attend my wedding in September 2018. This was the first time I had seen her in years.

Amanda looked drastically different than her old (pre-heroin) self but also appeared much healthier than she had been the previous year when she entered her last rehab. Some of her teeth had rotted from years of using heroin and meth, so she barely showed her teeth when she smiled. I could tell she was self-conscious about this. She had also gained back some weight, which was good. Her demeanor was calm, and she was a lot quieter than she used to be. I could tell she was really happy for me, though. I felt beyond grateful to have her there with my family—alive and sober. This felt like a miracle after all we had been through over the last couple of years. She brought a card to the wedding for Cort and me, and the words she wrote in it exceeded any and all expectations.

Amanda looked after my grandmother throughout their trip to Nashville. I think a part of her was trying to keep busy because Christopher's father did not let him make the trip down with my family to attend my wedding. I know this bothered her—hell, it upset all of us. I wanted him to be in my wedding as the ring bearer. He was my only nephew, and I hadn't seen him in a few years. It broke my heart that he missed out on this special day and time with my family. Amanda didn't bring him up much, but I know his absence was bothering her, too. She didn't like to talk about Christopher's father because she didn't like him and hated the fact that he had sole custody. However, I understood where Christopher's dad was coming from, being extra protective of him and not wanting him to travel out of state. This shit was hard to navigate. As a parent now myself, I can only imagine how difficult it would be to co-parent with someone with opioid addiction. Especially someone with a track record like Amanda's.

Speaking of which, after an amazing 2018, during which Amanda made leaps and bounds in recovery, she inevitably started to repeat her old behaviors. By December, Amanda started to act differently—similarly to how she'd acted during her last relapse the year before. I didn't hear from her as often, and whenever I did, she needed something from me. She would call me in a "huff," needing something right then and there, and if I couldn't deliver, she would angrily hang up or quickly say, "I gotta go." She started asking me to order her more Uber rides, and she never put in the effort to actually use the bus pass that my dad paid for every month. It was getting old.

She also wasn't opening up to me like she had been in previous months and often went days without calling. When I asked her if she was going to meetings, she got angry and said things like "When am I supposed to go to meetings? I'm always working and in so much pain from being on my feet all day. I'm exhausted, Nicole." There was always an excuse. And it was becoming apparent that recovery was not her top priority. Whenever she started acting this way, I could see the writing on the wall. And it was surely clear this time. It is important for a person in recovery to make *recovery* their number one priority. Amanda tended to start out strong with this mindset each time she discharged from rehab, but she always lost sight of it after a while. I believe this is a big part of the reason she failed at staying clean over and over again.

A few weeks before Christmas 2018, Amanda called to tell me she had gotten kicked out of her recovery house due to an issue over her gabapentin prescription. Apparently, she had been taking more than prescribed, and when the staff counted her pills, she was short for the month. This must not have been the whole story or not have been the first time this had happened. They don't just put you out on the street if you mess up in recovery houses. At the very least, they help you get back into rehab if you fail a drug test. They want you to succeed and will give you plenty of opportunities to correct your mistakes and/or go back to rehab if necessary. But at the time, I wasn't aware of these things, so when Amanda called me and told me this, I believed her.

I was skeptical of her story because she had been communicating with me less, but she sounded composed over the phone and promised she hadn't done any drugs. I really wanted to believe her. She explained that her pills were short because she sometimes needed an extra gabapentin or muscle relaxer to help manage her fibromyalgia pain. I was pissed that she was kicked out of yet another recovery house and didn't understand why her pattern of behavior was repeating itself again. She begged me for help, and I felt like I couldn't say no and leave her on the street if she really wasn't using hard drugs. I told her I would help her if she promised that she would continue to attend meetings and communicate with me regularly. She promised me she would do so, but I should've known better.

I helped Amanda rent a room in downtown Harrisburg. Apparently, this place wasn't in the best part of town, but it was what we could afford. After helping her get set up, I started hearing from her less and less leading up to Christmas. I knew she was going home to spend time with our family the week after Christmas and had a supervised visitation approved with Christopher. While I was home for Christmas, I tried to warn my mom that Amanda might not be doing well, but my mom never fully believed Amanda had relapsed until she heard it directly from Amanda. When I got back to Nashville, I waited to hear from my mom about how things went during Amanda's stay with my family.

I wasn't surprised to hear that it was a disaster. According to my mom, Amanda slept basically the entire time and barely paid any attention to Christopher. My mom had her ways of knowing my sister wasn't doing well, but she didn't always act on her intuition and instead would just fight with Amanda. It didn't take long before my mom called Amanda out about her lack of attention toward Christopher, which, of course, caused a fight. Then my stepdad got involved, and that always triggered

Amanda even more. She hated hearing his opinion and would fight him tooth and nail over everything. They could be arguing about whether the sky is blue, and it would be like World War III in our house. They were that repellent to one another.

They apparently fought during the entire trip to take Christopher back home—while Amanda was awake, that is. After hearing about this and about how badly my sister was acting, especially in front of her son, I knew she was using again. There was no question in my mind. The moment I heard that Amanda was sleeping all day when she finally had the opportunity to spend time with her son, I knew she was under the influence of *something*. With Amanda, nine times out of ten, that something was heroin. I didn't need any proof, failed drug tests, or her to admit it to me; I just *knew*.

I decided to handle this relapse a little differently, though. I knew if I confronted Amanda, she would be ashamed and not want to admit her mistakes. If I got upset and accused her of relapsing, she would be angry with me and not want to talk to me. I decided all I could do was reach out and hope that a judgment-free approach would be enough to get her to talk to me. I knew I couldn't be upset, angry, or judgmental. *I had to meet her where she was.* I decided to reach out to her with a gut-wrenching text message—something to grab her attention but show that I wasn't mad at her. I wanted her to know I was concerned but wouldn't be upset with her about anything if she talked to me. Luckily, this time, she decided to answer.

CHAPTER 10

A NEW APPROACH TO RELAPSE

I sent this exact text message to Amanda on January 24, 2019, at 10:56 p.m.: "Listen—I know you're not doing well. You don't need to pretend with me. I'm not mad at you, I just don't want to lose you. When you're ready to get yourself back on track, let me know and I'll try to help. But I will not enable you and I will not watch you continue to slip backwards into your hole. Don't let whatever happened or whatever slip up you had ruin all the progress you've made before it. You fall down, you get back up. That's how it goes. Screwing up does not mean you're a screw up. It means you're human—a human with a disease. That has ups and downs. You can either stay down and die from this one day, or you can get back up and fight for the life you know you want. Choice is yours. As always, I love you. And will always be there to support you in the RIGHT direction <3."

About ten minutes after I sent the message, she responded, "I really needed to hear this from you, I was going to reach out. I just haven't yet. Can you talk? I love you, Nicole." A few minutes later, Amanda called and proceeded to tell me about her relapse. She said, "I'm not real bad or anything. I scheduled my Vivitrol shot for Monday; I just need to get to York. It is vital that I get down there and then back, because I don't want to run into Shannon down there." She then thanked me for reaching out and said, "I feel like you're the only person who somewhat understands addiction in our family. Thank you for just being you and not giving up on me." I told Amanda I was proud of her for being so honest with me and I was happy she already had her Vivitrol shot scheduled. We hung up and promised to talk more the next day.

The next day, I heard from Amanda around 1:00 p.m. I had a break in between patients at work, so I was having lunch in the parking lot of a bagel shop when Amanda texted me. She said, "Hey, so I think I'm going to go stay in Carlisle, I don't even know this guy but he's willing to help me & take me to my appt on Monday." I stared at my phone, baffled, and pondered how to respond. I knew she probably didn't think this was the best idea, or she wouldn't have texted me about it.

I remained calm and decided to not to overreact or offer my opinion just yet. I simply responded, "What guy?"

"Some Mike guy I was gonna stay with. I have to move out of here today." (Meaning she had to move out of the house where she was renting a room, presumably because she wasn't going to be able to pay her rent.)

"How do you know him?"

"I don't. I met him on a dating app."

I didn't like the sound of this situation and really didn't feel comfortable with Amanda going to stay with a complete stranger. At this point, she still hadn't admitted she had relapsed to anyone but me. I thought about how I should respond and eventually went with "I'm not sure that's the best idea. I would prefer if you went back to a recovery house or, even better, back to rehab."

She quickly responded, "I can't go back into a recovery house yet because I don't have clean urine." Then, "I don't need rehab every time I mess up. There's nothing they can teach me that I don't already know."

I responded, "When will your urine be clean?"

"Monday."

"Will you be willing to go back to a recovery house after that?"

"Yes, I can go back on or after Monday when I can get my Vivitrol shot and pass a drug test."

I thought to myself, *Okay, no rehab, but we'll get her right back into a recovery house with accountability, regular drug screenings, and a supportive community. I can handle that.*

And that's what we did.

I played the facilitator between my sister, aunt, and parents. I was on and off the phone all day micromanaging my sister's affairs and living situation like I was her caseworker. I talked to my mom and told her about Amanda's relapse. Of course, she wasn't happy and seemed surprised despite the warning signs she had witnessed just a few weeks prior when Amanda was home visiting the week after Christmas. Nonetheless, I convinced my mom and stepdad to drive down, pick Amanda up, and bring her back home to their house for a few days until she could get her Vivitrol shot on Monday. Amanda agreed to this plan and thanked me for getting her the help she so desperately needed.

Using this supportive, loving, and judgment-free approach to her relapse was by far the best decision I ever made when it came to her addiction. There was some sort of divine power working through me that day, that's for sure. I don't know how I remained so calm or how I got her to open up to me, but for whatever reason, it worked, and I couldn't have been more grateful. This was truly the moment that everything changed between us. I believed this was going to be the time Amanda would finally change for good. I thought with my help and support, she could conquer anything.

We had to keep her relapse quiet because Amanda had just gained back some parental privileges with Christopher in 2018, during her long stretch of sobriety. This was part of the reason why she didn't want to go back to rehab. She would have to report this to the caseworkers involved, and she could lose all the progress she had made toward getting partial custody back. So, as long as Amanda agreed to get her Vivitrol shot on Monday and to go right back into a recovery house, I was okay with her keeping this within our family. She hadn't hurt anyone and hadn't put Christopher in any danger. She was being open and honest about her relapse for the very first time.

A few hours after Amanda and I first spoke, my mom and stepdad drove about an hour to pick her up. This was a big deal. For one, Amanda and my stepdad had horrible dynamics, as I've explained, and they never saw eye to eye on anything. Furthermore, my mom was always a nervous wreck dealing with anything involving Amanda's addiction. She hated the fact that Amanda had relapsed. Even though she could see the writing on the wall, my mom always believed my sister was clean up until the very minute she admitted she had relapsed.

It was tough for her as a parent; who wants to believe their kid is lying to them *yet again*? I couldn't blame my mom for not wanting to see the full truth even when it was right in front of her.

Amanda was honestly surprised that they were coming down to get her, and maybe even a little indifferent as well. She didn't want to hear a lecture from my stepdad the whole way home. I assured her that I had talked to both of them and clearly explained how embarrassed she felt about everything. They both promised to be supportive and not ask too many questions. Their main role was to simply provide Amanda with resources—somewhere to stay and a few hot meals—until we could get her back into a recovery house in a few days. I would take care of the rest and make sure she had somewhere to go after she got her Vivitrol shot on Monday.

My mom called me on the way home to let me know they had picked up Amanda and all of her belongings. She hadn't eaten in a few days, so they were stopping for food on the way home. I was happy to hear she was with them and the plan was working out so far. In the meantime, I called my dad to bring him up to speed with everything going on. He didn't have much to say, of course. He never did whenever Amanda relapsed.

I had learned over the years that everyone handles these things differently. I became the crisis worker, asking, "How can I help diffuse the situation?" and "What are the next steps we can take?" My mom turned into the worrier, asking too many questions, getting upset or angry, but never really offering any solutions to figure out the situation. And my dad became the fleer—he would retreat from all conflict and "hole up" until he was ready to talk. I knew my dad had dealt with a lot when Amanda lived with him for several years before her heroin addiction escalated, so I tried my best not to get upset with him. I knew in time he would come around and deal with the situation in his own way.

A few hours after they picked her up, my mom and stepdad brought Amanda back to their house and settled in. Amanda called me and told me that everything was going well so far. She was calm and sounded very clear over the phone, the best she had sounded in months. The difference between this phone call and the ones we'd had prior to her admitting she had relapsed were night and day. I was so proud of her.

During these few days before we got her back into a recovery house, Amanda and I had more honest and raw conversations than we had in years. Things just felt *different* this time. I thought we were going to repair our relationship, and with my support and open, honest communication, she was going to stay sober. I felt confident of this with every fiber of my being. I was so proud of her for owning her relapse, for being immediately open to getting help, and for being honest with me throughout the entire experience. This was truly a first in all the years of her heroin addiction, which, if you're keeping track, had been five years (her first overdose was in January 2014).

Things went well for those few days my sister spent with my mom and stepdad. I can only recall her calling me one time to complain because she wanted to go somewhere and they had told her no. I had to play the go-between again, but I didn't mind because Amanda was actually receptive, unlike previous times, when she'd fought the idea of having to stay in the house. And, of course, being told what to do. She was very stubborn, remember? But overall, one situation during a three-day stay with my parents was miraculous.

On Monday, my aunt drove Amanda down to York to receive her Vivitrol shot from her addiction doctor. I've since learned that you can only receive the Vivitrol shot if opioids are completely out of your system, so she was definitely clean at this point. We had worked together over the weekend to find her a recovery house that had a bed available and was still close to her addiction doctor. We had also prioritized finding one that would give her more structure, including accountability, requiring her to attend ninety meetings in ninety days and find and keep a job in order to stay. She had lost her job at the grocery store after getting kicked out of her last recovery house.

We decided she would go to a women's recovery house in Harrisburg, and I helped by paying the first few weeks of rent and security deposit. She actually was excited to go and seemed grateful for my help, both financial and with finding a place. It was weird having this relationship with her. Everything was different, but in a very good way. It was the Amanda I had always hoped we'd see in recovery.

After settling into her recovery house later that day, she called me right away to let me know things were going well. She made friends with her housemates and seemed to actually like them for a change. Things were off to a good start, and I was so excited that everything had worked out according to plan. This was the first time in five years that I could honestly say that.

I asked her to keep in touch with me daily and to fill me in on her progress and how things were going. She told me she would need to attend ninety meetings in ninety days and that she was excited to jump back into recovery. She was ready for whatever she needed to do to get her life back in order, and for the first time, *I actually believed her.*

CHAPTER 11

HISTORY REPEATING

The predictability and unpredictability of addiction go hand in hand. On one side, you're never really surprised by anything your loved one is doing. They repeat behaviors; they disappoint you. It's all part of the process. But at the same time, they show glimpses of hope. They make you believe in them all over again. You want to believe this time is the time they get sober and stay sober—until it isn't. And that part sucks.

I had been down this road with Amanda so many times by now, you would think there could be no more unpredictability. But as I have said, this relapse felt different. She made me believe in her again. The raw honesty between us was unlike anything I had ever experienced with her throughout the five years of her heroin addiction. I finally felt like we were on the same page. It was a beautiful and miraculous thing: two sisters were finally able to see things for what they were at the exact same time. No lies, no deceit. Just love and support for one another.

The circumstances around this relapse, in January 2019, may have clouded my judgment for some time. It wasn't all bad, and I don't mean to imply that, but looking back, there were some warning signs I may have missed. A few weeks after Amanda had settled into her new recovery house, she still hadn't found a job. I tried to be patient with her, as she was still being open and honest with me and keeping in touch daily. So, although I was disappointed she hadn't found a job yet, I didn't want to discourage her from what was most important: her recovery.

Eventually, Amanda told me she had found a job. She was going to work for a friend's husband, who owned a cleaning business. I thought this would be the perfect job for Amanda because she loved cleaning and—when she wasn't using—she was always very intentional about keeping her place clean.

She also gave the girls she lived with an opportunity to make some extra money, because her boss always needed extra people to help with cleaning jobs. The only concern was her attitude toward her boss. She had a problem with the way he treated his wife, who was a close friend from her previous recovery house. She claimed he was controlling and hadn't let her friend talk to her for months prior to this. "He feels threatened by our friendship," she would tell me. I didn't like the sound of this. Wherever there was drama, Amanda always knew how to escalate the situation.

A few weeks later, Amanda called me, upset and on the verge of tears. Apparently, her boss had let her go and said he wouldn't be needing her or her roommates' help anymore. He claimed there were issues with how many cigarette breaks they were taking and the thoroughness of their cleaning work. Amanda, however, refused to believe this. She said he'd let her go because he was not comfortable with the many late nights she and his wife were spending together while cleaning workplaces.

I really didn't know what to believe. This sounded fishy, considering everything Amanda had said about him prior. She was very upset that she had lost this job after putting so much into it and actually liking the work she was doing. She promised me she would find another job right away and already had a meeting scheduled with a woman who helps people in recovery find resources, including employment. I told her I would help her the best I could until she found a job, but that she needed to take things seriously. It was not easy for me to hand out money and trust that she was using it appropriately.

Looking back now, Amanda losing her job was the first incident I should have considered a red flag. However, I was easily persuaded to believe Amanda's story given the history between her and her boss. I also had to accept the hard reality that people in early recovery tend to lose a lot of jobs, and Amanda was no exception to that. I knew she was trying, and because this time in recovery had started off so much better between us, I was not ready to give up hope. I believed she was going to find a job soon and trusted the communication and strong relationship we had established after her last relapse. Unfortunately, this trust didn't last long. I wish I could say that Amanda's communication and recovery efforts stayed positive, but history tends to repeat itself, especially when things get hard.

I recently reread some of our text messages from this time, and I could feel the frustration on my end as Amanda began exhibiting the same behaviors she had during her prior relapses. For one, she had promised she would get a sponsor. After attempting to rekindle things with her previous sponsor and realizing that wasn't going to work out, instead of finding a new one, she basically gave up on NA altogether. This was frustrating, but no matter how many times I asked her about it, I couldn't make her go to meetings or do the work for her. She had to do it and want it herself. I learned this through Nar-Anon.

Amanda eventually found a new job at a Dollar General close enough to where she lived that she could walk to work. She didn't always walk, though, and rarely used her bus pass. I was regularly getting her Ubers to and from work, and it drove me crazy because she would barely give me a heads-up, and she expected me to have a car there for her within minutes.

Around March 2019, I noticed that she had started to talk to me differently. She wasn't as open and honest with me as she had been and would often call me upset about silly things again. Or she would only call me when she needed something. I started to think her behaviors could have something to do with the prescriptions she was taking, so I called her out on it. She played coy and asked, "What prescription do you think it could be?"

I did my research and found that the gabapentin she was taking in high doses could affect her mental clarity. I also found that it wasn't a good combination with one of her other medications, Flexeril, which she took for muscular pain. The combination of these drugs could cause dizziness, drowsiness, confusion, and difficulty concentrating. When I explained all of this to her, she assured me that she wasn't misusing any of her prescriptions and that both medications helped her fibromyalgia pain. She stressed that she didn't have many other options because she couldn't take opioids, obviously, and was already taking 800 milligrams of ibuprofen a few times per day as well. I eventually let it go, but I knew deep down that she was different than she had been back in January, when she wasn't on any medications.

Another issue that came up during this time was Amanda's use of online dating apps. She seemed to be staying out with a guy she had just "met" online almost every night of the week. I was concerned that she had replaced her addiction with sex instead of drugs, which can be common in recovery. If she had reflected on this while sober, Amanda would surely have admitted that was what she was doing, but at the time, it was a constant battle with her. I felt like I was always trying to remind her of why she was in the recovery house. I would say things like, "You are not staying in that house to just sleep around. You are supposed to be staying there at night instead of sleeping with random dudes." She denied having an issue or sleeping around, but I knew better.

Over the next several months, from March to May 2019, I watched as Amanda once again started showing signs of relapse. At the time, I was just beginning to think she would never be her old self, that her outbursts and selfish ways were just part of the new normal. I kept comparing her current behavior to her behavior in January after she relapsed, when we had so many wonderful moments and conversations together. I was convinced her prescription meds had changed her mentally, but she had no interest in getting off of them, so I tried to accept her new behaviors. I struggled with knowing when to pick my battles and knowing what was just normal "person-in-recovery behavior." She was never completely honest with me about her use of dating apps, where she was spending her money, or who she was spending her time with, so it was difficult to know how to trust her.

There were still plenty of good moments, though. She called me one morning, upset about some of her roommates' behaviors. She told me that some of the girls had relapsed, and one of them was high in the house the morning she called me. She sent me a picture of a girl who was nodding off while sitting on the couch. This girl looked like a mess. I said to Amanda, "You know, that's what you used to look like—and even worse sometimes. You should see some of the videos Mom sent me of you from two years ago."

She said, "I know, and I know I never want to look like that again. I have no interest in using drugs like that, Nicole. I promise you."

At times like these, I truly believed she might have changed. Sure, she was a little selfish sometimes and would often only call when she needed things, but she was still in early recovery. And, in all reality, what did I expect from her? But this *incident*, this *moment* when she called me and expressed how upset she felt seeing her roommates high, was progress in my eyes. Amanda was now considered a mother-like figure in this recovery house. This was the first time she had ever assumed that role. I was proud of her.

In May 2019, Amanda decided to do something for herself that she had long wanted to do. She scheduled dental work to remove her remaining natural teeth and replace them with a full set of top and bottom dentures. She had major self-esteem issues about her teeth because she barely had any left after years of heroin and methamphetamine use. For quite some time, she had built up the idea that getting her teeth out was going to be a life-altering experience and would boost her self-esteem and confidence. She thought it would heal her wounds and make her feel better about her appearance.

With Medicaid, Amanda's options of where she could have her dentures fully covered by insurance were limited.

Fortunately, she found a clinic that accepted her insurance plan, so she was able to have the extractions done and dentures made at no cost to her. After the procedure, Amanda was in pain, and I worried she might relapse because of this. She assured me that she told the clinic about her history of addiction and she was not prescribed narcotic pain medication. She was only taking ibuprofen. I thought about how hard having surgery must be for people in recovery from opioids. Essentially, they can't take prescription opioids for the rest of their lives, even if they're having elective surgery, as Amanda was in this case.

Luckily, Amanda managed her pain well using just ibuprofen. However, when it was time to have her denture fitting, she had some issues with how the dentures fit in her mouth. They were way too big, and she needed several follow-up appointments to adjust them. After the second or third appointment, things were finally turning around, and she was starting to get used to them. She sent me a picture on May 22, my thirtieth birthday: her with a big smile, flashing her new dentures and wishing me a happy birthday. I'm not going to lie—it was strange seeing her with those big fake teeth, but I figured they would just take some getting used to. Little did I know that she was also having a hard time adjusting, and despite trying to make the best of it, she was struggling with her appearance.

I later learned that having a major surgery such as teeth extractions during early recovery can impact sobriety. From the psychological effects of one's appearance changing to potentially needing narcotics for pain control or needing time off work, several large obstacles and setbacks may need to be overcome post-surgery at an already incredibly vulnerable time. I wish I had known and considered this so I could warn her, but unfortunately, Amanda had convinced me that getting her teeth out was exactly what she wanted. I only saw the positives in her decision because she had put so much emphasis on how getting dentures would be miraculous for her self-confidence. However, several weeks post-surgery, I was starting to doubt that she had made the right decision.

At the time, I was preoccupied with everything I had going on in my own life. My husband, Cort, had just taken a promotion and we were in the process of selling our house in Nashville and relocating to Tampa, Florida. I oversaw getting our house ready to sell and was busy every day with projects and coordinating with contractors to make necessary repairs and changes to the house. It was such a crazy time that I didn't have the mental capacity to deal with Amanda's issues, especially since a lot of them just involved her complaining about her teeth or asking me to get her an Uber somewhere. I needed to focus on myself and my family for a change.

Shortly after my birthday, communication between Amanda and me became inconsistent. Week after week, I sent her numerous texts, checking in on her to make sure she was okay. Some of my messages got replies; some didn't. I didn't have the time to worry about her as much as I usually would, and to be honest, I was burnt out from constantly having to be the one keeping tabs on her. She was a big girl. She had a job and was paying her own rent at her recovery house. I didn't have time to micromanage her life, and for once, I was focusing on myself. However, by the end of May, it became clear to me that Amanda was not doing well. She was barely responding to my texts, and I was only hearing from her occasionally. On Memorial Day, Cort and I drove our animals and some of our stuff down to Florida, where we would be staying in corporate housing until we closed on our new house a few weeks later. Since we had a long drive, I decided to reach out to her, as I had in January, and check in without getting upset.

I said, "Hey stranger. How are you doing?"

She responded quickly and said, "Hey! I've been better, wyd…" (Meaning "what you doing?" She always used these text abbreviations.)

"On my way to Florida. Cort and I are driving down with the animals."

"Are you moving there for good now?"

"I'm going back to Nashville next week for CMA fest and to meet with the movers. They are taking our stuff down on June 12. What is going on with you though?"

"I don't want you to get all upset, honestly I wasn't even gonna tell anybody in our family cuz I feel like a failure again but I'm alright now, I refuse to destroy my life. I got high a couple of times, I moved out of the house and I'm staying in Mechanicsburg right now. I'm not sure what to do about my job cuz idk how I'm gonna get there & home, I'm applying to Weis Markets today in Mechanicsburg. They're hiring & the pay is the same as the dollar store. I think I'm better off living outside the city. Getting my teeth out really fucked me up & I wasn't expecting that."

"Wait, what? When did you move out? If you wanna go down that road again, that's your prerogative but you have had everything set up for you to do well and here we are. And you didn't reach out to me at all. Where are you staying? With some dude? Have you been going to work? Like do you even still have your job? Did you get kicked out for being high?"

I was probably asking too many questions, but I wasn't expecting to hear all those things at once. She hadn't just relapsed; she had gotten kicked out of the house and was staying with someone in a new place altogether. It was overwhelming to say the least.

"Yes I still have a job. I'm supposed to work today 3–close, but idk how I'm getting there or home. Nicole you have no idea how much bullshit I dealt with at that house with people drinking and getting high. It was ridiculous. Yes I'm staying with a guy who offered to help me out cuz I wanna get my own room when I get my next paycheck. I'm not going to continue this. I refuse to lose what I've regained with my son."

Again, I had one too many questions. "When did you get high? And with who? Can that guy take you to work? You should probably go to work if you want to get a room somewhere. And are you still getting high? When's the last time you had your shot?"

"A couple times last week. Last time was Saturday and by myself. No, he doesn't drive. I want to go to work but idk how I'm gonna get there or home. I need my shot, I couldn't get it last week because I worked."

I felt torn. I reviewed our texts with my husband and talked things over with him. Of course, neither of us was surprised. But at least she was being honest. I had hope that this could turn out the same as it had in January if I remained calm and offered support instead of getting mad or upset.

I responded, "If you promise you're gonna make an appointment to get your shot, I'll get you an uber to work. How did getting kicked out of the house come about?"

"Yes, I need my shot. I'm supposed to call them this week, I just don't know how I'm going to get there and back. My friend

Andrew might be able to take me. Of course, I blew through my check. That's another reason why I don't want anything to do with that life anymore, but honestly ever since that shit with my roommates getting high, it has been on my mind and my self-esteem was shot when I got my teeth out. One of my roommates saw bags in my drawer and since I brought drugs into the house, even though I didn't get high there, I had to leave. But I wanted to leave anyway, if I had stayed, I would still be getting high."

"Well, I'm sure we can figure out a way for you to get your shot. But I need to know you have an appointment. You can't just give up the moment that shot wears off and you're feeling bad about yourself. I appreciate you telling me. I'm not gonna run and tell mom bc she's doing too well right now to worry about this."

"Alright I will call them right now to schedule an appointment."

Later that day, I ordered Amanda Ubers to and from work. I tried to put myself in her shoes and really think about how hard it must have been to be around her housemates who had relapsed. And not only was she triggered by seeing them getting high, she had also recently had oral surgery and was dealing with her new image and learning how to care for dentures. I tried to remind myself that relapse was normal and part of recovery. She was recovering from substance use disorder with minimal coping skills, and using was the natural crutch to go back to.

I wasn't mad at her. As I had in January, I kept an open mind and was patient with her, especially in those first few days after she told me about her relapse. I wanted her to know she could trust me, and hopefully, we could get her right back into recovery like we had just a few months prior. She asked me not to tell anyone else in the family. Based on how things had gone back in January and how well she was communicating with me, I felt like I could do that for her.

As I have said before, relapse is part of recovery. I was learning how to deal with relapse just like Amanda was. She was learning how to be honest with me and how to trust someone who didn't also have a history of addiction to help her. Despite my frustrations, I was optimistic that we could get her back on track as long as she was willing. It wouldn't be easy, and it would take a lot of work, but I believed that as long as we openly communicated with each other, we could figure things out as we had after her last relapse. History tends to repeat itself, and I was hopeful this time would be no different.

CHAPTER 12

HISTORY NOT REPEATING

After Amanda admitted that she had relapsed in May 2019, I assumed we would get her right back on track, just like we had back in January. She was communicating with me, she still had her job, and she had already scheduled an appointment to get her Vivitrol shot. Compared to last time, we were ahead of the game. There was only one problem: her recovery house had kicked her out after they discovered she was using. Amanda didn't share this with me or anyone else until several days afterward. Instead of reaching out and asking for help, she decided to stay with a random guy she had met online until she could get herself together. After her last relapse she had reached out to me before she made the decision to stay with a stranger, but this time she was too embarrassed to tell me and thought she had everything under control. Until she didn't.

According to Amanda, the guy she met online said she could stay there until she had somewhere else to go. We still planned for her to get her Vivitrol shot in a few days, and I trusted that she would follow through with that. I was trying to treat her like an adult and not micromanage her life as long as she was communicating with me. She had a roof over her head for now, and I had a lot on my plate as well.

I was preparing to head back to Nashville for CMA Fest with my girlfriends, and then I would be meeting with a moving company a few days later to have all of my and my husband's stuff transported down to Florida. I was busy and didn't have time to worry about Amanda's every move. Of course, it bothered me that she had relapsed. But we had a plan worked out, similar to last time, and I was counting on her to hold up her end of that plan.

About a week before I was heading to Nashville, Amanda told me she needed to be out of the house she was staying in by the end of the week. I believe this was a Tuesday, and the guy she was staying with told her she had until Friday to find somewhere else to go. She didn't tell me any of the details about why or what happened, but looking back now, I assume her drug use was a big part of it. She knew how busy I was down in Florida, getting ready to move into our new house as well as managing things from a distance to sell our Nashville house. The Friday deadline didn't give us much time to figure things out, so I knew I would probably have to help her out financially to secure a place. But I made sure she knew *it was up to her to find the place.* I told her that whenever she got herself settled, it was time to seriously get back into recovery. I said, "I can't do it for you, so I will not preach to the choir. You know what you have to do."

She said, "I know; I love you. I'll call you tomorrow."

The next day, she started asking me for money. After taking some time to think about it, I told her I would send her money, but she needed to send me all her receipts, with dates and times, and pictures of what she bought. My trust in her was fleeting, and at this point it was hard to trust myself to send her anything. I didn't want to be the one to blame if she bought drugs and overdosed. I sent her some money via the Western Union app, and a few hours later she sent me some receipts of the food and cigarettes she had bought at the store. I also sent her some info on a recovery program to look into because I just couldn't help myself. Even though I was swamped with stuff going on in my own life, I cared so much for Amanda that I defaulted back to doing some research for her. However, I still put the responsibility on her to take the initiative in securing her next place to live.

By Friday of that week, I had purchased over one hundred dollars in Uber rides for Amanda to get to and from work. She still hadn't figured out where she was staying and was supposed to be out of the guy's house later that evening. On Friday night, she asked me to get her an Uber back to that same guy's house and told me she would call me in the morning. I asked her where she was going and what her plans were.

She responded, "Idk, somewhere close to my job."

"Well, where?"

"I'm not 100% sure, I'll call you tomorrow when I wake up."

I didn't answer. I felt like talking to her was a lost cause. I decided to give up and figured that if she didn't give a shit, then neither did I.

The next day, Saturday, June 1, she texted me, freaking out because she had nowhere to go and needed to be out of this guy's place by 6:00 p.m. She said, "Yes, I will go to another recovery house, I completely agree with you but I want to wait until I get my shot." Then she explained that another guy, Vic, would let her stay with him, but he lived further outside of the city, in Carlisle, so it would be even more of a hike for her to get to and from work. At this point, I was fed up with her. And I was over trying to remain calm.

I messaged her back. "I don't know what to tell you, Amanda. You knew you had to be out of there and you got yourself into this mess. You probably used again since Monday and don't have clean urine yet. I tried telling you since Tuesday that you needed to look for a place to go, but you haven't made any moves to do so apparently. If you get paid next week and can afford a place then, you should be able to make it work for a week."

"Nicole, I have nowhere to go. I'll figure it out, if I end up in Carlisle jobless at least I know Vic won't let anything happen to me. I gotta go. I'll talk to you later. I love you."

"I love you too, but I can't keep bailing you out, otherwise how are you ever going to learn from your mistakes? Let me know that you're safe. I can try to get you to work as long you're straight and get your shot."

A few hours later, I heard from her again. "Nicole idk what to do, I have nowhere to go. I am freaking the fuck out."

"I thought you were going to Vic's? Why don't you ask if you can go back to the house for the night?" (Meaning her recovery house.)

"Cuz it doesn't work like that. I don't wanna leave my job."

"What happened to staying with Vic"?

"I just told you I don't wanna quit my job or move to Carlisle. Like I have to leave here NOW."

"I'm not getting you a hotel, Amanda. I've told you that since Wednesday."

I didn't want to get her a hotel because I knew exactly what she would do in a hotel. She would lie around, use drugs, and do nothing to find herself a place to stay. I was done supporting her and spending all of our hard-earned money on Uber rides and hotel stays. I had made up my mind a while ago that I was only going to support her if she was in *active* recovery—not blowing her money on drugs or wasting her life away in a hotel room.

"Well I'm on the streets then." She was the queen of making me feel guilty.

"I've told you to look for a place to live and you haven't even tried. Don't put this on me if you are. This is your fault that you're in this situation in the first place."

"I don't have no money. I'm just fucking done, I'm sorry I can't do this anymore."

I was *furious* at this point. She had once again backed me into a corner and left me with no choice but to help her. My parents still didn't even know she had relapsed. "You can't do what, Amanda? Why are you in this situation in the first place? Because you fucking gave up. You expect me to bail you out of every situation. I asked you to call the recovery house or be willing to go to one. You said you had plans with Vic so I'm guessing they fell through. I don't even know what to believe at this point. I'm about to be at a dinner with Cort's co-worker and his family. I can't deal with all of this right now so you better figure something out."

"Figure out what, Nicole? I have NOWHERE to go. I know I fucked up, but I can't take it back now and I have nowhere to go. NOWHERE."

I didn't know what to think or to believe. Talk about a moral crisis—or just the everyday life of a family member of someone with addiction. Should I leave my sister on the street and hope she learns another lesson from all of this or help her out so she can keep her job and hopefully get back into recovery the following week? None of this was my fault, but I was somehow responsible for all of it. Suddenly, my sister's immediate future was in my hands. I had tried to put her in the driver's seat. I had tried to make *her* the responsible one. But I had failed. She didn't care enough to put the effort in. I thought she was clean, but she was quickly proving me wrong.

"This whole situation literally makes me sick, Amanda. I have done so much for you and you continue to put me in these situations."

"I know I hate myself, I'm nothing but a fuck up."

"Well then knock it the fuck off. I'm so tired of this Amanda, you have no idea. What the fuck do you want me to do right now?"

"I know. I feel horrible. Idk but I gotta be outta here by 6 & I have nowhere to go."

I hated *everything* about this situation, but I felt like I had no other choice. I talked to my husband and decided to give her one last chance to get herself together. I told her, "This is the last time I am doing this. You have until Tuesday to find a recovery house. I am not helping you find one, this is on you. If you have nowhere to go come Tuesday because you haven't looked for a place, then you're on the streets."

"Okay. I promise I will look for one."

"Is there a hotel near your work somewhere that you can go? Look it up and I'll get you an Uber there. And I'll get you the room for three nights. Then that's it. And I FUCKING MEAN IT."

"Thank you so much."

A minute later, she sent me a Google Maps listing for a local Howard Johnson hotel, where I would pay for her to stay for the next three days.

Little did I know, this would be the last place Amanda would call home.

CHAPTER 13

SHE HAS TO SAVE HERSELF

It's hard to find the words to tell this story. I struggle knowing I could have done more, could've asked more questions, could've stayed more on top of things. But I also know it wasn't my responsibility to do those things. It wasn't my battle to fight. It was Amanda's.

Sunday morning, June 2, the day after Amanda checked in to the hotel, things seemed to be heading in the right direction. At this point, I had already communicated with my mom about the situation, but I told her not to worry because I had things handled. And I really thought I did. Amanda was scheduled to get her Vivitrol shot on Tuesday. She worked Sunday, and I finally did not have to Uber her there because she was within walking distance at the hotel.

On Monday, June 3, she told me she tried to Facetime Christopher and was upset because his dad wasn't available when she tried calling. She also texted me information about a new recovery house and said she planned on reaching out to them. I thought we were moving in a positive direction.

The next day, June 4, she was scheduled to get her Vivitrol shot. This was also supposed to be her last day in the hotel, but a friend helped her pay for another night so she could worry about getting her shot and hopefully find a place to go the next day. The addiction specialist who oversaw her treatment was located about a half hour away from where she was staying. She didn't have a car, but she had a friend who was willing to take her there. She asked me for gas money to give to her friend since she didn't get paid for a few more days. I sent her forty dollars via Western Union and trusted she would use it for transportation to get her shot.

Later that day, I followed up with her a few hours after her scheduled appointment to make sure she had gotten her shot. She told me she had gotten it, was at work, and would call me when she was finished. Several hours later, I still hadn't heard from her, so I tried calling a few times. She finally got back to me and asked for an Uber ride back to the hotel because it was late and she didn't feel like walking. Of course, I helped her out with that.

Wednesday morning, June 5, she called and said, "I think I have pink eye and need to go to urgent care. I've never had pink eye before, but it really feels like it. I can barely open my eye." I was on my way to the airport for CMA Fest and to finish up the last bit of packing before the movers came the following Monday, June 10. I didn't have time to follow up immediately, but I messaged her later that afternoon, asking if she had gone to urgent care. She never answered me.

On Thursday morning, I woke up frustrated and worried once again. Amanda had never gotten back to me on Wednesday, and it was now two days past the original three-night hotel stay

I had paid for. I didn't know how she paid for the previous day or what she was going to do when it was time to check out of the hotel around 11:00 a.m. I texted her around 10:30 a.m. to see what was going on. "So, what's going on? Never heard back from you yesterday. Did you talk to the woman from the recovery house?"

A few minutes later, she texted me back. "I didn't wake up until late last night and went right back to bed. My eye is driving me crazy. I'm gonna go get my check soon & probably stay here one more night. No one is going to let me go anywhere today with pink eye. I will call her when I get back from cashing my check. I don't want to pay to stay here another night, but I don't have any of my stuff packed yet."

I thought to myself, *Okay, that answer checks out. She sounds appropriate, and she covered everything I was worried about.* But something in my gut still made me hesitate. I responded, "Okay. Please be honest with me though, did you get high?"

A few minutes later she texted, "Sorry I was on the phone with the hotel. No, I didn't. I'm extremely uncomfortable with my eye, my mouth, and my body's sore." Something told me she wasn't telling the full truth, but I decided to let it go.

I didn't hear from Amanda for the rest of the day, Thursday, June 6. I started to worry about where she was going to stay because she hadn't mentioned any solid plans to me at any point throughout the week. Despite my best efforts to stay out of it, earlier that week I had reached out to the recovery house that Amanda had mentioned to me on Monday. I talked to them about Amanda's situation and how we were looking to transition her quickly. On Friday, June 7, I received an email that they had been in contact with Amanda after playing phone tag for a few days. Amanda had never told me about any of their communication, so this was news to me. The woman said she explained their very structured program to Amanda, who said she would talk to me about it and get back to her. Amanda had yet to contact me about anything regarding the program, so I was irritated at this point.

I was ready and willing to pay for Amanda to get into this program. I had told her that as long as she was in a recovery program I would help her, and I 100-percent meant that. Yet she was communicating with this woman, not filling me in about any of it, and not following through with the plan we had established on Saturday, when I had initially checked her into the hotel. It was now Friday, June 7, and I was further out of the loop than I had been at the beginning of the week, and I had no idea what her plans were or how she was continuing to pay to stay at this hotel.

After I saw the email from this woman at the recovery house, I forwarded it to Amanda and then texted her "CHECK YOUR EMAIL."

She didn't respond. A few hours later, I texted again.

"What the hell is going on with you the last 3 days?? I'm done helping you if you're gonna shut me out."

I can still feel the agony and heaviness in my chest after sending those texts. It was Friday afternoon, and I was trying to enjoy myself at CMA Fest with my friends, yet all I could think about was Amanda. *Where was she? What was she doing? Was she using? What were her plans? How has she been paying for this hotel if she just got paid yesterday? Where is she going to go next?* I just couldn't stop thinking about her.

After receiving no response to my texts, I finally couldn't take it anymore and decided to call her. I stood outside the

Country Music Hall of Fame in downtown Nashville, accompanied by my best friend from Pennsylvania, who had traveled down to stay with me for CMA Fest. She knew I was struggling and gave me the space I needed to make the call. I called *three times* before Amanda finally answered. It was after 2:00 p.m., so she should have been awake, but it sounded like I had just woken her up. She shouted over the phone, "Hello? *What?* Nicole?" She sounded *horrible*.

I was upset with her, but I tried to remain calm because I knew that if I didn't, she would hang up on me. I asked her what she had been up to for the last three days. She mumbled some words about her teeth and told me she didn't feel good. I knew right away she had been using. I started crying and said, "Do you have any idea what you are doing to me? I am in Nashville trying to enjoy myself with my friends, and all I can think about is you. I worry about you every second, and you don't even have the decency to return my texts or calls. What is going on with you, Amanda?" She again tried to blame things on her "pink eye," her teeth bothering her still, and not feeling well overall. I knew she was lying and decided to confront her about getting her shot.

"Amanda, there is no sense lying to me. I know you're not clean, so please don't try to pretend that you are. Did you or did you not get your Vivitrol shot on Tuesday?" She finally admitted that she hadn't. "No, I decided I want to get on Suboxone instead. I have an appointment on Monday." Even though I had already assumed she had skipped out on her shot, hearing her admit it felt like the ultimate betrayal. I had trusted her and given her gas money to get down to see her doctor. I was also shocked that she'd said she wanted to get on Suboxone.

Amanda had been on and off Suboxone for years after she got off narcotic pain medication and before she ever tried heroin. Although I now understand how effective Suboxone is for many people in recovery, I didn't trust her on it. At the time, I worried she was just replacing her heroin addiction with another substance. And I recalled Amanda's grogginess and absentminded interactions with me during the years she was taking Suboxone, presumably because she was overusing it. Now she was telling me she was getting back on Suboxone after all these years, despite raving about how well Vivitrol worked for her. I was disappointed, to say the least, but decided not to ask too many questions.

Instead, I focused on the question I'd been asking myself for days. "Where do you plan on staying since you are still using?"

"I have no idea and don't know how I'm going to pay for this hotel. But I know you aren't going to give me any money now. I'll figure it out, Nicole."

I ended the conversation in tears. I told her I loved her and asked her to keep in touch with me over the weekend so that I would know she was still alive and okay. I was worried that she wouldn't make it through the weekend to see the Suboxone doctor on Monday, but I didn't know what else to say. I couldn't force her to stay clean or go into treatment. I had done all I could do.

Amanda promised she would keep in touch with me over the weekend and let me know she was okay. I hung up the phone with her and told my friend about everything that had happened. I tried to remain calm, but I knew things were not looking good for Amanda. I didn't know what else to do or say other than inform my family members that she was actively using again. I kept Amanda's relapse a secret, only telling my mom up to this point, because she had promised me she was getting her shot and was willing to go back into a recovery house. However, when she bailed on that plan, I bailed on keeping her relapse a secret any longer.

I called my aunt shortly after hanging up with Amanda and filled her in on everything. I knew that if Amanda needed money for the hotel or more drugs, she would be reaching out to her next. I then messaged my mom and dad to let them know the same, so they would know not to give her money. It felt like the same situation we had been in a year or so earlier, when Amanda was staying in the hotel with her ex-girlfriend, Shannon. She would eventually need money to keep staying at this hotel, or she would be stuck on the street. And we all knew Amanda would never choose to stay on the street. Cutting her off had been the best strategy then, and maybe it could be the best strategy now. All we could do was hope and pray that she would make it through until she needed money and reached out for help. That was the only way to get her back into treatment.

For the rest of the day, I couldn't shake the horrible feeling in my chest. The anxiety I felt was insurmountable. It felt like a sharp ache in my chest that was bubbling up into my throat. It was hard for me to focus and be present with my friends. All I could think about was Amanda. I didn't know what to do or how to fix the situation; I felt hopeless. For the first time in over five years, I truly felt I had lost my sister, and I had to be okay with letting her go. This was hard to accept, but the knowledge of this wouldn't go away. I had to sit with it all day, yet go through the motions as if nothing was bothering me. It was impossible.

I somehow managed to make it through the day and night portions of CMA Fest. Afterwards, my girlfriends and I walked downtown to have drinks like we normally do after the shows. I barely made it through one drink before the tears started welling up in my eyes. I felt like I couldn't breathe. One of my girlfriends saw me struggling and pulled me aside to chat and help me sort out my feelings.

I told her about the conversation I'd had with Amanda earlier and how hopeless and uncertain I felt. I didn't know if Amanda was going to make it through the night, let alone to her appointment on Monday to get Suboxone. Plus, I was pissed that she even considered getting on Suboxone in the first place. She was supposed to get her Vivitrol shot three days ago! It was sickening to me how backwards things had gone since she had first told me she relapsed, just a little over a week ago. How did things get this way? I could barely process everything, let alone try to think through these things while in a crowded bar with loud music in downtown Nashville. My girlfriend and I decided that I should go home. It was just too much for me to be in a public place in my current state. I said goodbye to the rest of my friends and took an Uber home.

When I got home, I let the emotion come over me. I lay on the couch for a few hours and played the same song on repeat. I couldn't stop the tears from flowing. It was all too much for me. Amanda had gone from communicating with me and promising she would find a recovery house to betraying my trust and lying to me about getting her Vivitrol shot. How the fuck did we get here? How in the world were we going to fix this? I didn't know where to turn or what to do. Part of me was grieving the fact that I had to let this go and release the small amount of control I was clinging to. Amanda chose this for herself. This wasn't her first relapse, and it probably wouldn't be her last. I had given her so much over the last few years. From money and countless Uber rides to finding her treatment options and micromanaging my family, I had done everything I could to help my sister, and she still wanted to use drugs.

In my brief time attending Nar-Anon meetings, I learned you have to "detach with love." And I knew that was what I needed to do here. I couldn't keep giving if I was constantly getting the same results from Amanda. Over and over again, I would help get her back into recovery and she would start off well, saying and doing all the right things to meet the criteria for admission. A few months would pass, and her whole attitude would change. She would stop going to meetings, stop caring about her recovery, and forfeit all the progress she had made over the previous months.

At this point, the vicious, repetitive cycle would only continue if we kept enabling her. I had tried to put the responsibility on *her* by asking *her* to find a new recovery program. She not only failed to follow through on that, but she also skipped out on getting her Vivitrol shot altogether. Her actions proved that she wasn't ready to put in the work to truly change.

For those of you who are struggling with your loved one's addiction, ask them this: "If I do *this* for you, will you do *this* for me?" If they say no, you have your answer. They aren't ready to change. And as we all know, unfortunately we can't do it for them.

I had to accept my own reality here: No matter how hard I tried, I couldn't save my sister. *She had to save herself.*

CHAPTER 14

WHERE IS SHE?

After a rough night of crying and constant worrying about Amanda, I woke up feeling a little better on Saturday morning, June 8. I had purged a lot of built-up emotions through my tears, so I felt that I was finally able to breathe. I also had a better understanding of how I was feeling and knew in my heart that I had done all that I could to help Amanda. I made it through the day and was happy to see that—at night, while I was at one of the shows—Amanda had texted me to let me know she was safe and wanted to have a long talk with me the next day. This gave me hope that she was still in there and considering getting some help other than just taking Suboxone.

However, Sunday, June 9, came and went without Amanda reaching out to me. The movers were coming to the house first thing Monday morning, so I focused more on being ready for them and less on Amanda's whereabouts. I had my concerns, of course. I had no idea where she was staying at this point or—if she was still at the hotel—how she was affording the room. But she had made her decision and chosen drugs over having my support. I had accepted that, and for once I was focused on my own life. In regard to her recovery, the ball was in her court. *I couldn't play for her anymore.*

Monday and Tuesday were both super busy with the movers packing up the house. I finished up last-minute projects and tried to stay out of the movers' way as they packed up our furniture and loaded everything up. I didn't hear from Amanda on Monday, and as much as I was focused on myself, I was starting to worry. I texted her on Tuesday morning: "I don't know what you're doing or why you're choosing to go down this path you're on, but I hope you realize the consequences of the decisions you're making. Because I promise you, eventually they will catch up with you." She never responded.

The night of Tuesday, June 11, I decided to call the hotel to see if Amanda was still staying there. The woman who answered the phone was vague, as if she didn't want to tell me either way. I tried my best to express that I was concerned for Amanda's welfare and told her I was the one who had paid for her to be in the hotel in the first place. I also wanted to make sure my credit card was not being charged if she was still staying here. The woman confirmed over the phone that she did not see an active reservation in Amanda's name, so she must have checked out. I took this as an interesting sign, but a good one. At least I knew she was somewhere else, and because she hadn't called any of us asking for money, I knew she wasn't out on the streets.

By Wednesday, June 12, I still hadn't heard from Amanda. It was my last day in Nashville, and I was preparing to fly out later that night after the movers finished up. I tried my best not to worry about her, but the longer the silence went on, the more challenging this became.

That afternoon, my mom called me with some unsettling news. "Nicole, Shannon just reached out to me on Facebook and is concerned about Amanda. She hasn't heard from her in a few days and said it's very unlike Amanda to stop answering her. She said yesterday was her birthday and Amanda didn't even reach out to wish her a happy birthday."

And just like that, the ache in my chest and all the anxiety returned. I took a deep breath and tried my best to stay calm for my mom. I asked her several questions, which she relayed to Shannon as they corresponded over Facebook Messenger. After a few minutes, I told her to have Shannon call me so I could get a better sense of the situation.

Within minutes, my phone was ringing. Shannon sounded concerned when I answered the phone. She was speed-talking as she recalled the details of the last few days. "Nicole, I don't know how to say this, but I am concerned about Amanda. It's very unlike her to not answer my calls or texts. Earlier this week, she was falling out almost every night. She is using fentanyl, and that shit fucks you up. I wouldn't mess with that—it's too risky. The other night, I had to stay on the phone with her for over an hour to keep her awake and make sure she didn't OD. I just don't understand why she would be doing this. She was doing so good and had worked so hard to get Christopher back in her life. It just makes me so sad. Even though we're not together anymore, we always keep in touch. I feel somewhat responsible for making sure she's okay, you know? All those times she Oded before, I was always there to save her. Now I'm worried it's too late."

It was a lot to take in at once. I processed what she had told me, and immediately the panic started to build up in my chest. I tried my best to breathe so I could continue this conversation and get more information. "Where do you think she is, Shannon? Where was the last place you knew she was?"

"Honestly, Nicole, she was at the hotel until at least Monday. That's when I stopped hearing from her."

"The hotel I helped her get? The Howard Johnson?"

"Yes, as far as I know. My friend Christine helped her pay for one of the nights last week. Amanda promised she would pay her back and then stopped answering her phone."

"Do you know if she is with anyone else now?"

"I know she was hanging out with some guys I've never heard of. I don't know if they could have done something to her. But I'm really worried, Nicole. I really think something happened to her."

"Okay, thank you, Shannon. And thank you for reaching out to my mom. I know we've had our differences in the past, but we really appreciate you letting us know this."

"Of course."

"We're obviously concerned about Amanda. I tried my best to help her, but she lied to me and decided not to get her Vivitrol shot. She couldn't stop using, I guess. And now knowing that she's using straight fentanyl scares the shit out of me."

"I know. Me too, Nicole. I wouldn't touch that shit. I always test my stuff to make sure it's not laced with it. It's everywhere now, honestly, and more people are dying. I'm really worried about Amanda. I'm sorry, and I wish there was more I could've done."

"Thank you. I'll be in touch if I hear anything."

"Okay. Thank you. I'll let you know if I hear anything, too."

After speaking with Shannon, I decided to reach out to several of Amanda's friends and a few of her old housemates to see if they could give me any information. My heart raced as I typed out a message to one of her housemates, Tasha. I was desperate for any information. "Hi, I'm really sorry to bother you. I know you were at the recovery house with my sister, Amanda Davis. Any chance you have any idea where she could be? Or could you try to get in touch with her for me and see if she answers? She has gone AWOL and we haven't heard from her in days. Really just want to know if she's alive."

I couldn't believe it had gotten to the point of sending out these messages to strangers, but I had to collect as much information as I could so I would know what to do next. Tasha responded to me quickly, but unfortunately didn't have much information to share. She said, "The last time I heard from her was Saturday night. I just sent her a text, I'll let you know if I hear anything. Where is she staying?"

I responded, "Thank you so much. That was the last time I heard from her too. She sent me a text Saturday night saying she was safe but that was it. She was in a hotel. I called and they say she's not there anymore. Not sure where she is or who she could be with. She said all kinds of names I didn't know. She was supposed to get her shot last Tuesday and bailed for some reason."

"Oh man, I'm so sorry. I don't understand what happened. I will try reaching out a few times. I'll let you know if I hear anything. I'll ask the other girls too."

"Okay, thank you. Appreciate your help."

I called my aunt next. "Hey Anne Marie, when did you last hear from Amanda?"

"Hang on, let me check…It was late Monday night. She sent me a text, but it didn't make any sense. I tried calling her yesterday, too, but no answer all day. I don't know what she could be doing."

"Okay, yeah, seems like that's the last anyone has heard from her. Shannon just reached out to my mom. She's concerned because she hasn't heard from Amanda or been able to reach her since early Monday herself. She said it was her birthday yesterday and it was very unlike Amanda not to wish her a happy birthday."

"Jesus. Maybe we can see if there's anyone on Facebook from down there who might know where she is."

"One step ahead of you."

"Let me know if you hear anything."

"Okay."

I received a few messages back from some of Amanda's other friends, but no one had heard from her since Saturday or Sunday. Any attempt to find Amanda was coming up empty. I felt defeated. I called my mom back and we both decided it was probably time to contact the police. No one had heard from Amanda since Monday. We learned she had been using IV fentanyl and her last known location was the hotel. I was starting to panic, thinking that she might have overdosed.

After gathering all of this information and reaching out to Amanda several more times myself, I decided to file a missing person's report with the local police in Harrisburg on Wednesday, June 12. This was not how I expected to be spending the last day in my Nashville home. I sat on my bed, one of the few things not yet packed up, and dialed the number for the Swatara Township police station, the closest precinct to Amanda's last known whereabouts: the Howard Johnson hotel.

I waited a few minutes before a dispatcher answered. I zoned out, staring at the wall while waiting on hold. How could this be real life? I was starting to feel really guilty. Had I done enough to help my sister? I just wanted all of this to go away.

When the dispatcher answered, I gave her all of my sister's basic information: her date of birth, last residential address, and last known whereabouts. I told her it had been about forty-eight hours since anyone in our family had heard from her. She asked me detailed questions about Amanda's appearance, physical and mental health, and habits and personality. I answered the questions to the best of my knowledge, and after about a half hour, she said, "Okay, an officer will be contacting you shortly for more information. Thank you." I was so overwhelmed. I couldn't believe this was our reality right now.

I couldn't stand to be alone by myself thinking about all of this, so I called my friend Kim and asked if I could come over to distract myself. We sat in her living room as I explained everything that was going on. I couldn't wrap my head around this reality, and verbalizing all of it out loud was excruciating. I called Amanda's phone every fifteen minutes, praying she would answer, but it would ring and go to voicemail every single time. Finally, an officer called me while I was at Kim's house, and I explained the situation to him in more detail. I told him about Amanda's history of drug use, the last time anyone had heard from her, and how this was very unlike her, considering we had cut her off financially. I told him her last known whereabouts was the Howard Johnson hotel and her place of employment was the Dollar General. He told me he would check out both places and get back to me with an update when he had more information.

I stayed at Kim's house for a while, until I had to pack up my stuff and leave for the airport. As I processed everything that was going on, I felt comforted in knowing she was there for me. Cort was in Tampa working, so it was difficult going through this without my husband there to lean on. Later that evening, as I was about to leave for the airport, I finally heard back from the officer. He said he had stopped by the Howard Johnson, and they didn't have an active reservation in the system for her, which was what they told me on Tuesday when I called. He said they were checking paper copies of receipts to confirm when she checked out, but it seemed like their filing system was a complete mess. He said he also stopped by her work and a few other local places, but no one had seen her. He promised he would keep an eye out and update me when he had more information. I thanked him and told him I would let him know if there were any updates on my end as well. I tried my best to hold it together as I headed to the airport and said goodbye to my Nashville home.

Later that night, I landed in Tampa. Cort picked me up at the airport, and we headed to the corporate housing apartment where we were staying. I barely slept all night as I replayed the events of the day in my mind and continued to worry about Amanda. The next day, Thursday, June 13, I called her phone over and over and over again. I felt the tension build as I waited to hear if there would be a ringtone on the other end, but at this point, calls were going straight to voicemail. "Hey, it's Amanda. I can't get to the phone right now, so leave a message and I'll call you back. Thanks." I left a few messages, but after a while, I figured what was the point? I knew she wasn't getting the messages, yet every time I called, I couldn't help but feel a glimmer of hope that her phone might start ringing.

I was in agony all day as I waited to hear something—
anything—that might give us some hope, or at least some
answers about what was going on. One of my girlfriends
reached out to offer support. She suggested that Amanda
could possibly be caught up in sex trafficking in exchange for
drug money, as young women, especially those who are addicted to drugs, are often targeted by men and other women
caught up in trafficking. This was something I had thought
about briefly after hearing Shannon say that Amanda was
hanging out with some sketchy guys she had never heard of.
It also made sense that this could be a possibility if Amanda
truly did leave the hotel and was staying somewhere else. Sex
traffickers will lure victims by offering a place to stay, money,
clothing, and drugs. Amanda was vulnerable due to wanting to
avoid detox symptoms and was limited on cash, so I could see
this as a possible scenario. Of course, it was concerning, but I
preferred to consider this situation rather than the alternative.
At least in this case, Amanda would still be alive and we could
possibly save her.

My friend gave me the number of a man who was highly
involved in raising awareness about trafficking and finding
and rescuing victims. I texted him and explained the situation. I said, "Hi, I got your number from my friend, Stacy. I
know this is a long shot, but my sister Amanda is missing. I
think she could possibly be involved in trafficking. Is there
any information you can give me?" He responded quickly and
called me a few minutes later. We had a good conversation,
and I learned a lot from him about how these scenarios work.
Illegal drugs, such as opioids, are an ideal component of a
successful human trafficking operation. Sex traffickers often

target people with substance abuse disorders with the promise of unlimited drugs to keep their victims under control. Once the traffickers have their victims, they take away their phones, and it's possible that the victims' families never see or hear from them again.

This scared the shit out of me, but also gave me hope that Amanda could still be alive. The man was going to do some digging and said he would get back to me with any information he could find.

Around 5:00 p.m., I finally heard back from the police officer working Amanda's case. He didn't have any updates for me, but he wanted to know my current address. I was confused about why this was pertinent information and was pissed that he didn't have any new updates. Was he still even looking for her? I was annoyed, but I explained to the officer that I was no longer living at the Tennessee address I had given the dispatcher the day before. I told him I'd flown to Florida last night and was staying temporarily at an apartment until we moved into our new home. He asked me for the address at the apartment, which caught me off guard. Why did he need this new address when we were only staying there temporarily? If this was for paperwork reasons, why couldn't he just use the address at our Nashville home? I complied nonetheless and gave him the address. He thanked me and said he would be in touch.

About an hour later, I told Cort that I could not stay in the apartment any longer without answers. I was literally going *crazy* and kept replaying worst-case scenario after worst-case scenario in my head. He looked at me and said, "Come on, let's get out of here for a bit. Let's go grab dinner."

I hesitated at first, but then thought this might be a nice break from reality. I said, "Okay, let's go." We walked hand in hand to Bulla, a tapas place within walking distance of the apartment. We laughed, ate, drank a bottle of red wine, and walked home in a brief moment of peace.

After we got back to the apartment, it was only a matter of minutes before my phone started ringing. It was a Pennsylvania number. I figured it was the police officer calling to give me an update. I wish it had been the officer. In my version of this story that I wish I could rewrite, it would be the officer calling to tell me they had found my sister alive and safe. Unfortunately, this was not the case—and this was the moment my entire life changed forever.

CHAPTER 15

THERE'S NO WAKING UP FROM THIS NIGHTMARE

"Hello?" I answered the call anxiously.

"Hi. Is this Nicole?"

"Yes, this is she."

"Hi, my name is Lisa, and I'm with Dauphin County. Nicole, I'm calling because you had filed a missing person's report with the Swatara Township Police, and I have your number as the primary contact."

"Okay…"

"Are you at home, or are you driving or anything?"

"Yeah…My husband and I just got home."

"Okay, good. Well…Nicole, we think we found your sister, Amanda. Can you tell me, Nicole, does she have any tattoos?"

I stumbled over my words as I recalled where her tattoo was located. "Yes, uh, um, it's on one of her wrists. Uh, it says her son's name and, uh, his birthday. Um, 2/21/08." I felt my heart pounding through my chest.

"Okay, thank you, Nicole. I am with the coroner's office. I am so sorry to tell you this, but I responded to a call at the Howard Johnson hotel on Eisenhower Boulevard around five o'clock this evening. They found Amanda there in the hotel room. It looks like an accidental overdose, but we have been having a hard time getting an adequate urine sample for accurate toxicology results. So we will likely need an autopsy in order to confirm this."

Tears started welling up in my eyes. I couldn't believe this. My heart raced as I attempted to find words in response to the coroner. "Oh my god. I can't believe this. Oh my god."

"I know. I am so sorry."

"How was she still in that hotel? I don't understand; they said she checked out."

"Honestly, we're not sure either. Apparently, there had been a mix-up with the cleaning system, and they never got back to her room to clean it. So they didn't know she was in there. They found her this evening."

"Wow. This is unreal…I can't believe this. Oh my god. I'm sorry; I'm just in shock right now."

"It's okay. Don't apologize. But I need to get some more information."

"Okay…uh, yeah…Whatever you need."

"Where do your parents live, Nicole? I want to send officers out to them to let them know what happened."

"You want to send officers to their houses? What? I think they'd rather hear it from me, don't you think?"

"That's up to you, ma'am. But I recommend sending the officers just in case. We like to notify next of kin in person in case something were to happen, like a medical event. The officers will be there in person if needed."

At this point, Cort walked over to me. He had been listening; I'd answered the call on speakerphone. He put his hand on my shoulder. He looked at me and said, with concern in his voice, "I don't think you should have to be the one to tell them, Nicole. Don't put that burden on yourself. You'll never forget having to say those words to your parents for the rest of your life." I looked at him out of the corner of my eye and nodded my head in agreement. I hadn't even considered that. I didn't feel great about having this knowledge and not being able to immediately call my mom and dad, but at the same time, I was traumatized and in shock. Cort and the coroner both thought I should send officers out for different reasons, but both reasons were valid. It was one of the hardest decisions I've ever had to make, but I decided to let the police tell my parents.

I recited my parents' names and addresses to the coroner over the phone. She said she would send officers out soon to notify them, and she put me on a brief hold. After a few minutes, she came back on the line and said local officers had been notified and would be going to my parents' homes soon. She then asked if I had any questions for her. I thought to myself, *Where do I even begin?* I had so many questions, but I felt shellshocked. I was in full fight-or-flight mode at this point—it was hard for me to even process the idea of a question.

After a minute that felt like an eternity, I fumbled out some words. "Sorry...I'm just in such shock right now. Do you know if there was, um, anyone with her who could have possibly left her there?"

"Possibly," she responded. "Based on initial evidence, it doesn't look that way. But we can't confirm or rule that out yet at this point."

"Okay…Um, do you know how much she used? And it was heroin, I'm assuming?"

"Well, we found nine bags in the room of what looks like fentanyl. It was a white powdery substance. There were four bags used, one half used, and four unused and unopened."

"Oh wow. That sounds like a lot."

"It is. Especially for fentanyl. But it's hard to say if she used all of this at one time. We'll have more of an answer on that when we do the autopsy."

"Okay, so you're definitely going to do an autopsy?"

"I'll let you know for sure, but it looks like it. We have tried multiple times to get urine, and we just can't get any at this point."

"Oh wow, okay. Um, uh…man, I just can't believe this. She was sober for a while and was doing so good. She just recently relapsed. As far as I know, she's never even used fentanyl before. I just can't believe this."

"I know, Nicole. I'm so sorry. We found all of her sobriety tags from NA in her purse. It looks like she had a decent stretch of sobriety there. Unfortunately, that's how a lot of these overdoses happen, though—after a relapse. The body just isn't used to the drug anymore, and it's often too much for them to handle."

"I know. She did have a long stretch; that's why this is so shocking to me. She was supposed to get her Vivitrol shot last week. I thought she was getting back on track. I trusted her. I put her in that hotel room with the plan to transition to a recovery house. I don't know why she did this. I just don't understand."

"I know, and I'm so sorry."

"Thank you. Do you know when it happened—when she died? Is there any way to tell?"

"It's hard to say, exactly. When we find a body, there's a formula we use to determine the approximate time of death, but it gets tricky if it's been longer than twelve hours. She's definitely been there longer than twelve hours; I can confirm that. If I had to guess, I would probably say two days. So, likely sometime on Tuesday, maybe even late Monday. But it's hard to know for certain."

"Wow. Okay, well yeah…that timeline does add up based on the last time someone heard from her."

"Yes, and another thing I want to mention, Nicole, is how we found her. Because of the way her body was positioned when she died, what we call 'livor mortis' caused significant discoloring in her face. So, depending on the type of service you and your family want to have, you probably won't be able to have an open casket."

"Oh. Wow. Uh, what do you mean?"

"Well, Miss Amanda was found in a position where her head was below her heart. Her legs were behind her and tucked back almost in like a frog position with her bottom in the air. After the heart stops beating, after a while, blood starts to pool in the lowest part of the body relative to the heart. Gravity naturally causes this to happen. So, Amanda's face, unfortunately, was the lowest part when we found her."

"Oh. Okay…"

I started shaking. This was a little too much for me to handle. It was bizarre to me how casual this conversation seemed to be for the coroner. But I was not ready to hear these details and now could not get this image out of my head.

"But the funeral director can give you more clarity on that when we release her body. They are able to work wonders with makeup these days, so it's possible she could still have an open casket."

"Okay, yeah, I haven't even thought about any of this. I'll have to talk to my parents."

"Yes, of course. I just wanted to let you know so you're not caught off guard later."

"Well, thank you. I appreciate that, I guess."

"Do you have any other questions for me?" the coroner asked.

At this point, I was overwhelmed. Cops were on their way to tell my parents Amanda had died. The coroner had just described *in detail* how they found my sister when I was not prepared to hear this information. I was all out of questions at this point. I was more worried about my parents and whether the police had been to their houses yet.

"No, I think that's about all I can take for now. Thank you for all the information."

"Yes, of course. Feel free to take my number. Have one of your parents, or both, call me with any questions. I would like to speak to one of them tonight, if possible. I called you because you were the contact on the missing person's report, but I would like to speak to one of your parents."

"Okay, I'll pass that along when I hear from them."

"Thank you, Nicole. And again, I'm so sorry."

I hung up the phone, and all of a sudden, I was shot back into my body, sitting in our living room at the apartment. I looked at Cort, finally making eye contact with him, my eyes wide open, expressing my shock about what just happened. I tried to stand up, but immediately my legs gave out from underneath me. I sat back down, buried my face into my hands, and let out the loudest sob I had ever heard in my thirty years of life. Uncontrollably, I bawled hysterically. This was my worst nightmare, and it had just come true. Cort sat next to me and wrapped his arms around me. He sat and listened to me scream and cry, rubbing my back and offering me tissues. I had never felt this type of pain before. It felt like something inside of me had died.

When I was finally able to catch my breath, I sipped some water and sat on the edge of the sofa, perched over the coffee table as I stared at my phone, waiting for it to ring. I figured the police had to have gotten to my parents by now, or would be getting there soon. I waited in agony to hear from either my mom or dad, not knowing who would get the news first. Those were the longest twenty minutes of my life. When my mom finally called me, I sobbed as I answered the phone. "Hi Mom…"

"Hi. Do you know, Nicole?" she asked quietly.

"Yes. I'm so sorry, Mom…" I sniffed and tried to catch my breath. "I didn't know what else to do. They wanted me to send the police."

"Well, I wish you hadn't. That was the worst moment of my life." She wasn't crying—she sounded angry.

"I'm sorry, Mom. I wanted to tell you, but they told me not to. They wanted me to send the officers to you."

"Well, I wish you hadn't. I knew exactly what it meant when the doorbell rang. It was traumatizing, and I'll never forget that moment for the rest of my life. I've feared that call or that moment for how many years, and it just happened."

"I'm sorry, Mom. I didn't know what to do."

"Well, what's done is done now, Nicole. What are we going to do? Does your dad know?"

"I haven't heard from him yet."

"Well, let me know when you do. I have to call the coroner, I guess."

"What did they tell you?"

"Not much, really. They just said they found her at the hotel, and I need to call this Lisa person right away. So…uh, do you know what happened?"

"Yeah, I can fill you in somewhat before you call her…"

I proceeded to tell my mom about my conversation with the coroner. I tried to recall everything I could remember: how they found her, how I had to identify her by the tattoo on her wrist, and how they thought it was fentanyl. I explained that they were having a difficult time getting urine, so they would likely need to do an autopsy. I tried to remember everything I could, but I was still in shock, so the details were escaping me. My mom was definitely in shock, too—and angry. She kept saying, "I can't believe this. I should have gone down to get her; this wouldn't have happened. Like last time, when Keith and I went down for her."

"Mom, you can't do that to yourself. Who knows? If you had gone down and gotten her, it could have happened in your house!"

"Well, at least I would have tried…"

"I know. I'm sorry, Mom. I really did try. We had a plan figured out. She was supposed to get her Vivitrol shot. I told you this last week. I don't know why she didn't. But I feel like I did everything that I could. And I'm still so confused how she was still in the hotel. They said she had checked out when I called. And the cop went there the next day looking for her, and they said the same thing to him. I don't understand how she could have been in that hotel room the entire time…"

"I don't know either, Nicole. If she was still in there, why couldn't they go check that room? It doesn't make any sense. Well, I guess I'd better call this Lisa."

"Okay, call me after you talk to her."

"Okay."

I hung up with my mom and waited anxiously to hear from my dad. I waited for over an hour, staring at my phone. There was no way the cops hadn't gotten to him yet. What was taking so long? I decided I couldn't wait any longer and texted my dad and stepmom. I asked them to call me right away. My stepmom called me a few minutes later, concerned. "Nicole, honey, what's going on?"

"Mary, are you with my dad?"

"No, honey, I was out. He's asleep. What's up? Do I need to wake him up?"

"Yes…" I paused. "I'm so sorry, Mary, but yes."

"Okay, it's okay, Nicole. No worries. Just give me a minute."

I could hear her walking through the house as she worked her way upstairs to their bedroom to wake up my dad. I heard her say, "Jerry, Nicole's on the phone." He mumbled as he woke up.

A minute later, Mary said, "Okay, Nicole. We're both here."

"What's up?" my dad mumbled.

I took a deep breath. My voice cracked as I cried out, "I'm so sorry, Dad…"

"What happened?" he immediately asked.

I did my best to form a coherent sentence. "They found Amanda tonight at the hotel. The coroner called me a little over an hour ago. She tried sending out officers to tell you in person."

"Oh my god, honey. Nicole, I'm so sorry," Mary said.

I heard my dad getting choked up. "I knew it," he murmured.

"I'm so sorry, Dad."

"Me too, Nicole. Did you talk to your mom?"

"Yes, she knows. The cops told her. She's not too happy about that. But she's on the phone with the coroner now. You can call her, too, if you want to ask some questions."

"No, I'm good. But I'll call you back. I need to call my boss and let him know I won't be in tonight."

"Okay."

We hung up the phone. And once again, I let out a deep, guttural sob. *Why the fuck did this happen? Why did I have to be the one to tell my dad?* I will never forget that moment for the rest of my life. Telling your parents that your only sibling just passed away is something I wouldn't wish on anyone. Drug overdose was something we all knew was a possibility, but none of us ever wanted to believe it would be our reality. All of a sudden, this possibility was our real life. *There was no waking up from this nightmare.*

CHAPTER 16

SEARCHING FOR ANSWERS

In the days that passed, I found it hard to take in everything going on around me. I lived in an alternate universe, with each passing moment feeling more unreal. I was lucky enough to make it through each day without completely losing my shit. I was holding on by a thread.

The first few days were by far the hardest. Even eating a meal felt like a daunting task. The day after we found out, Cort and I decided some fresh air would do us some good, so we walked across the street to have lunch at a sandwich shop. As we sat outside and ate our lunch, I took deep breaths and managed to hold it together for a while. I had messages coming in like crazy from friends, family, and Amanda's friends on Facebook, but I tried my best to stay present and take a break from my phone. I just sat and breathed and took small bites of my meal.

Reality quickly set in, though. I heard a Tom Petty song playing over the restaurant's speakers, and for some reason, it triggered me. I have no idea why, but as I heard the chorus of

"Here Comes My Girl," all I could think about was Amanda. Suddenly, I lost the ability to breathe. My stomach felt like it was coming up into my throat. The first major wave of grief crashed over me as I sat with my eyes closed. The tears started flowing. I began hyperventilating and needed to leave immediately. The overwhelm came over me so fast, I never even saw it coming.

I've since learned this is often how grief hits us: when we least expect it.

A few days later, I flew home to be with my family and prepare for Amanda's memorial service. My mom was taking things really hard and playing the blame game. This made me uncomfortable because I was the primary one in contact with Amanda toward the end, and I wasn't ready to take on guilt on top of my grief. That was too much for me to handle. I thought I had done all I could to help Amanda, but now I was second-guessing myself.

It was challenging for me to even have a conversation with my mom during these first few days because of how unstable she was. I couldn't blame her, though. I didn't know what it felt like to lose a child, and I hope I never do. I tried to hold space for her and let her grieve in her own way, in her own time. That was all I could do.

I started planning Amanda's memorial service with Mark, one of my dad's best friends, who owns a funeral home. My parents and I decided to have her cremated and planned the service for Saturday, June 22. I communicated with Mark several times that week to help pick out flowers and determine other things involved in the service. I once again had assumed the responsibility of handling things for my sister. I guess I just couldn't help myself.

The days leading up to the service were hard. My aunt and I drove down to the hotel where my sister had died to talk with the hotel staff and collect any items she had left behind. My aunt and her friend had already been there once to clean and pack up whatever items were worth saving. I was hesitant to go into the hotel, but I knew it would be good for me to see.

As we entered the lobby, an overwhelming feeling came over me. This was the hotel that I had put her in just a few weeks prior. I had called them on the phone and paid for her to stay there, thinking it would be a short three-day stay. Never in my wildest dreams did I picture myself walking into this lobby a few weeks later to enter the scene of my sister's death.

The woman working at the front desk greeted us kindly. She gave us a key to the room and said we could take as much time as we needed. The hotel staff had left everything untouched, as they wanted to make sure the police were finished investigating before they cleared the room.

As we walked into the room, I noticed the musty smell of stale cigarettes. I saw Amanda's clothes still hanging in the closet located right inside the door. There were things all over the room, including cigarette butts, ashes, food wrappers, and clothing. It was hard to believe that my aunt and her friend had already been there once to clean up. They must've walked into a tornado the first time.

I walked around the room and tried to get a sense of what had happened. It was hard to imagine living like she had been living, out of bags and large containers where she kept her things as she moved from recovery house to recovery house. I knelt down to look underneath the bed and smelled something quite unpleasant coming from the carpet. I don't know what

I was trying to do, but I found myself searching all around the room for some sort of answer. Unfortunately, the answer never came.

The cops had already picked up any remnants of drugs that were in the hotel room. The only thing I found related to any sort of drug use was a muscle relaxant pill underneath the bed. I had to Google what it was, of course, and found there was a moderate interaction with opioids that could lead to slowed breathing and extreme sleepiness. This didn't surprise me, as both drugs slow down the central nervous system. We didn't know exactly what other medications Amanda was taking and what other interactions could have been at play.

My aunt and I did one last sweep of the room before we left. As I was about to leave, I noticed a sweatshirt hanging with Amanda's other clothes. It was an old hoodie with a picture of Notorious B.I.G. and a young Jay-Z on the front. This stood out to me; I couldn't shake the memory of a young Amanda playing "I'll Be Missing You" by Puff Daddy, a song written about Notorious B.I.G. after he passed. This felt like a symbol that Amanda was still with us. I thought about taking the hoodie with me but decided I would leave it. Everything was still too fresh for me at the moment, and I felt too fragile to have something of hers that was also in the room where she died. (My aunt has since gone back for this hoodie.)

We left her room and went down to talk to the front desk clerk. I wanted answers because I didn't understand how Amanda was found in that room on Thursday, June 13, almost a week after she had supposedly "checked out." According to hotel staff records, Amanda had checked out of the hotel on Friday, June 7, which was also the last time I had spoken to

Amanda over the phone. I struggled to understand how she was in there the whole time and why they just couldn't go to *her room* and check from the very beginning.

The woman at the front desk explained that on Friday, June 7, Amanda came to her and asked if she could do a late checkout. The woman said yes and that she could pay for a half day and leave the key in the room after she left. Amanda paid her the half-day rate and went on her way. The woman didn't think much of it and assumed Amanda had left later that day.

The next day, the room was supposed to be cleaned by housekeeping, but it was skipped due to not being reserved by a guest. The woman at the front desk claimed there must have been a glitch in their system, because the room somehow disappeared from their "to be cleaned list" for several days and did not reappear until Wednesday of the following week. When staff attempted to clean the room on Wednesday, June 12, they found that the door was bolted shut from the inside, so they could not get in. They called maintenance to open the door so the room could be cleaned. However, for some reason, that didn't happen on Wednesday, which was the day the officer stopped by the hotel to look for Amanda. Instead of letting him see which room she was in, so he could see for himself that the door was obviously still locked from the inside, they told him she had checked out and searched for paper receipts to prove this.

The following day, Thursday, June 13, my sister's hotel room was somehow listed as "clean and ready for guest" in the cleaning log records. However, the room was never actually cleaned because the maintenance man hadn't come to break open the door until earlier that day. The front desk clerk was not aware of this and issued this room to a new guest. When this guest arrived at the room and opened the door, he saw my sister's clothing hanging inside the closet located immediately to the left of the door—and thank god for this. He turned around, went back to the front desk, and told them he needed a different room because someone else's belongings were in there. Had this man walked further into the room, he would have found my sister in there, dead on the floor. Instead, it was the housekeepers who found her after the front desk clerk sent them in to check out what was going on with this room and why it was listed as clean and ready to reserve.

The front desk clerk told us the housekeepers did not initially realize what they had found. They thought Amanda's body was a blow-up doll. She said, "People tend to frequent this hotel and do weird things, so it would not be uncommon for our housekeepers to find a blow-up doll in one of the rooms. The girls told me what they had found, and I needed to go see for myself." She paused for a moment, as she took in my and my aunt's wide-eyed expressions. Then she continued: "I knew immediately that she was not a blow-up doll and called 911 right away." She cleared her throat. "I am so very sorry."

She apologized to me and my aunt over and over again for the events that transpired leading up to her finding my sister on Thursday, June 13. As much as I appreciated her apology and understood it wasn't her fault, I couldn't help but wonder what could've happened if someone had actually checked on her room and asked her to leave after she was supposed to check out. Remember, she had initially checked in on June 1 and supposedly checked out June 7, but her body wasn't found until June 13, despite the police officer having visited the hotel on June 12. I couldn't comprehend how a person could be in a hotel room for almost a week after they had supposedly done a "late checkout" without any hotel staff knowing. What would have happened if they had actually gone to clean the room the following morning and told her she had to leave? Would Amanda have called me and told me she was ready to get help? I guess we'll never know, but I can't blame the hotel staff for Amanda's actions. They weren't the ones sticking the needle in her arm.

After we left the hotel, my aunt and I stopped by the local police station to see if we could meet with the detective who was on duty the night they found my sister. Luckily, he was there and met with us for a few minutes to answer our questions. He started by telling us how confused he was by the mix-up with the cleaning services at the hotel. He didn't understand how everything played out the way it did and apologized for that, even though it wasn't his fault. He described what they found in the hotel room with Amanda. He said there were several used and unused bags of fentanyl as well as several needles, including one that was found underneath her. At this point, we still didn't have an official autopsy report and wouldn't have that for another week or so, but we all knew what had happened to Amanda. She had clearly overdosed, and now we had confirmation that it was from fentanyl, not heroin.

The detective explained that these days, most of the so-called heroin on the streets in Harrisburg is actually fentanyl. And if it isn't pure fentanyl, it's heroin laced with fentanyl. What they had found in Amanda's room looked like pure fentanyl, judging by its color, which he described as powdery white, not a tar-like substance, as heroin typically is. This information got my head swirling.

I started thinking about a conversation I had with Amanda about a month and a half earlier. She had called me and was upset that one of her housemates was using again. She wasn't just upset because she was using, but because of *what she was using*, which was *fentanyl*. She told me she didn't understand how anyone could gamble on their life like that and how the majority of overdoses are caused by fentanyl or heroin laced with it, which is what she believed caused several of her overdoses in the past. How did Amanda go from being completely upset by the actions of one of her housemates using IV fentanyl to using it herself? I'll never get an answer to this question; it will leave me wondering for the rest of my life.

The police were holding on to her phone and laptop as evidence to conduct a criminal investigation. I learned during this process that the person who sold Amanda the fentanyl could be charged with homicide, as overdose cases are now considered homicides in Pennsylvania. I wanted justice and answers, so initially, I wanted the police to do whatever they could to get into Amanda's phone and give us some clarity on what had happened.

This situation turned out to be more complicated than that, and they were never successful in finding out who sold my sister her fateful dose of fentanyl. Looking back on it now, though, I think that's the way Amanda would have wanted it. She wouldn't have wanted someone else taking the fall for her actions.

Later that day, we went through Amanda's belongings that my aunt and her friend had picked up from the hotel room during their initial cleanup. This was a lot harder than I thought it would be. I wasn't ready to do it, but I felt that

I didn't have a choice. I had to be there for my family. And I didn't want my mom to be stuck doing this.

Amanda had quite the collection of belongings, but was actually pretty organized, with file folders and calendars. She had saved a ton of stuff from over the years, including birthday cards, pictures of family and friends, and drawings from Christopher. She had calendars filled out with dates of upcoming doctor's appointments and friends' and family members' birthdays. She also had a lot of financial documents and written lists detailing the debts she owed to various financial lenders.

I kept several things we had found in my sister's stuff, including old letters she received from friends in jail, several of her calendars, and a few of her file folders that I planned to go through. I found myself pulling at strings trying to understand Amanda better. I wanted to understand what she had been going through. I wanted to understand the shit she never shared with us because she didn't think she could or didn't feel comfortable doing so. I wanted to know the secrets of her life. I needed answers, and I was willing to do whatever digging and research it would take to find them. I wish I could say the answers were there waiting for me, but unfortunately, they were not.

We also went through a ton of clothing, and I helped sort out what was worth keeping and what we should get rid of. I knew my mom might want some things because she and Amanda were relatively the same size. I used my best judgment to make these decisions, as Mom wasn't ready to go through these things herself. In one of the containers, I found the dress Amanda had worn to my wedding less than a year earlier. I decided this would be the one sentimental item I would keep, and it's hanging in my closet to this very day.

We spent the next few days preparing for Amanda's memorial service. I printed a ton of photos, ordered collages and picture frames, and spent the day before the service putting everything together. Many of her old friends, whom she had lost touch with, had held on to photos and gave them to our family to use at her service. The night before the service, I spent time with old friends and family, going through pictures and reminiscing on memories from our childhood. It was unbelievable to see Amanda's transformation from a young girl, and even in her high school and college days, to the person she was when she passed. It is remarkable what drugs can do to a person, not only mentally and emotionally, but to their physical appearance. Despite all of this, I tried to focus on the good times, the photos with positive memories, and the pictures Amanda would have wanted on display at her memorial. I knew she would want to be remembered as the beautiful girl she once was.

CHAPTER 17

IN MEMORIAM

On the day of Amanda's memorial service, I woke up with a knot in the pit of my stomach. I knew this day was coming, but that didn't make it any easier when it finally arrived. I felt conflicted. Traditionally, funerals and memorials are supposed to be a "celebration of life"—but how do you celebrate the life of your sister who just overdosed on fentanyl? How do you celebrate a life that was so up and down, back and forth, and in constant turmoil? How do you look past the messiness of her drug use and celebrate the human being underneath it all? Meanwhile, I was grieving and still processing the fact that she was gone. It was a lot to take in. I felt suffocated.

I did my best to get dressed and put on a good face for my parents. My husband and I drove to the funeral home alone. We didn't talk much on the way there; it was hard to find the right words or make small talk in such a somber moment. My dad was waiting for me at the funeral home. Christopher arrived soon after, accompanied by his dad and stepmom. This was the first time I had seen Christopher or his dad in several years. I hadn't expected his dad to attend, but I appreciated him being there for Christopher. After watching them interact for a few moments, I could see the bond they had formed together over the last few years. This was comforting to see, knowing he had support from his dad and stepmom. I fought back tears as I watched them from a distance. I had been so busy preparing for this day, I hadn't taken the time to think about what all this meant for Christopher. I wasn't ready to face him, but I knew I had to. I felt horrible that it had been years since I had last seen him and that I was seeing him under such dire circumstances.

Christopher ran over to me. I wrapped him in a big hug, and we embraced for several minutes. I wasn't prepared for this moment; so many thoughts ran through my head. *How do I ask him how he's doing? How do I hold space for him while allowing myself to grieve?* As hard as all of this already was, it became significantly more complicated. As we embraced and my mind wandered to all of these thoughts, I squeezed him and told him numerous times how much I loved him. After a few minutes, I finally looked down at his now taller figure. I wiped the tears from my eyes and smiled. "Wow, buddy. You've gotten so big!"

He gave me a half smile. "I know, Aunt Nicki. I'm eleven now."

"And I can't believe that."

He smiled.

"I'm so sorry, bud…for everything."

"I know," he said quietly, looking down at the floor.

"Your mommy was very sick for a long time. But she loved you so much. Please don't ever forget that."

"I know. I won't."

Christopher seemed to only partially understand, but I didn't want to disclose any more details on a day that was already filled with so much sadness. "C'mon. Let's go look at some pictures of Aunt Nicki and your mommy from when we were little."

"Okay."

Hand in hand, we walked over to look at some of the memory boards and pictures of Amanda. Out of the corner of my eye, I saw Christopher's dad walk over to us. I turned and gave him a hug and thanked him for coming. He gave me a nod and said, "I wanted to be here for him. He needs us right now."

I nodded in agreement. "Yes, he does." Christopher proceeded to show me his cremation necklace, which his dad had ordered for him and sent to the funeral home so that Amanda's ashes could be placed inside of it. I said, "Wow, that is really nice. And now your mommy can be with you all the time." He looked down at his necklace and smiled in agreement.

Of the many family members and friends who stopped by that day, Christopher was the hardest to embrace. My heart ached every time I looked at him. I wasn't sure how much his dad had told him about the situation or how much I should openly say about the nature of Amanda's passing. Of course, now that I'm writing this book, one day he'll have a better understanding. But that entire day was heart-wrenching.

The memorial service started. Guests started to arrive, but my mom still hadn't shown up yet, and I worried that she wasn't going to. I was told to stand at the front with the rest of my family so people could pay their respects. My dad, Christopher, and I made our way to the front of the room near my sister's urn, which was on display. This was the first time I had ever stood at the front of the room at a viewing. I had never lost anyone this close to me before, and it felt strange that people were stopping

by to give their condolences to me. With each embrace, I tee-
tered between breaking down and holding it together.

Shortly after the start of the service, my mom finally arrived. She was hanging on by a thread; I could see it all over her
face. On top of attending my sister's service, my mom was also
dealing with the stress of my grandmother's declining health.
Unfortunately, my grandmother had recently been admitted
to the hospital and was having a very untimely triple bypass
surgery at the same time as Amanda's service. The universe
was quite literally testing my mom's strength on this day. I
prayed desperately that my grandmother would make it out
of surgery, alive and in better health. My mom couldn't handle
much more at this point.

I watched as several people embraced my mom as soon as
she entered. Always so polite, my mom hugged everyone who
approached her before she made her way to us at the front of the
room. She joined my dad, Christopher, and me as people continued to line up and offer their condolences. My stepdad, Keith,
joined Cort and my stepmom, Mary, to stand at the front, but off
to the side. They let our core family have our moment together.

After the line of people stopped, the four of us—me, my
dad, my mom, and Christopher—stood facing Amanda's urn,
arms wrapped around each other. For several minutes, we just
stood there and embraced, letting the tears flow and acknowl-
edging our sadness. I'll never forget this moment for the rest
of my life. Although this was the saddest moment of my life,
the love I felt between the four of us was unlike anything I had
ever experienced. I can linger in that memory forever.

Soon it was time for the priest to start the service. I thought
about speaking about Amanda's life and how much I loved her,

but I just couldn't bring myself to do it. It was hard enough being there and feeling the energy of everyone mourning in the room. I couldn't imagine speaking and trying to hold myself together in front of my family and some of my closest friends. Looking back, I'm happy I made this decision because I'm not sure that what I would have said that day would be how I truly feel. Writing this book, recounting her story, and looking back at the memories have given me a much broader and more impactful way of remembering her. Her memorial service would not have been the right platform to speak about my feelings surrounding Amanda's life, death, and battle with addiction.

The truth is, I was still in shock and simply holding myself together for my family. The way I had learned about Amanda's death was traumatic, and I had not yet even begun to process my feelings or emotions. As I write this now, two years after Amanda's death, I have done the work and healing so I can now speak with clarity. And while I don't consider myself an expert on addiction or recovering from trauma, I have learned and grown so much since the day of Amanda's memorial service. Now I see the broader picture and understand the significance of sharing Amanda's story to help destigmatize conversations surrounding addiction and its effects on family systems. As I've mentioned, Amanda and I planned on writing a book together one day to share the events of this story from two perspectives: that of the person with substance use disorder and that of a family member. Although we couldn't see that through, I know now more than ever that sharing my side of the story, as a sibling, is important. As much as it hurts to share some of the details, I know there are many lessons to be learned from my experience.

CHAPTER 18

LESSONS

How do I remember my sister? How do I honor her life and everything she went through to show that her life had meaning and was important? How do I demonstrate the significance of addiction issues and how they impact families every single day? The best way I know to honor Amanda and ensure her life has a lasting impact is through telling her story, and that's exactly what I've chosen to do in this book.

As much as Amanda drove me crazy, I loved her *so much*. I truly hoped that one day she would find the strength to overcome her addiction. She worked hard to get as far as she did, and I recognize the struggle she had, especially in the end; I'll just never quite understand it. I'll never understand why she didn't get her Vivitrol shot or why she chose to keep using when she had my financial support to get back into treatment or into another recovery house. I'll never understand why she chose drugs over her son. She had worked so hard to get herself together and had finally earned supervised overnight visitation with Christopher at my mom's house once per month. She had one overnight visitation with Christopher in May before she passed away in June 2019. *One.*

I know Amanda didn't want the life of an addict; she told me this so many times throughout her recovery. She hated the person she became while she was using; yet her addiction controlled her life. Opioids shackled her to a life she despised but couldn't get away from. As her sibling, I'll never quite understand that, because my brain is not wired like hers. I never had that switch in my head that I couldn't turn off or even the urge to make the leap from partying to using hard drugs. For this, I am truly grateful because I have learned that a person with addiction would switch places with me any day to have that self-control.

I know now, more than ever, that addiction is an illness. Not a choice. And I will advocate for that stance for the rest of my life. According to the NIDA, the Substance Abuse and Mental Health Services Administration (SAMHSA), and the National Institutes of Health (NIH), drug addiction is considered a disease because it causes long-term changes in how the brain responds to situations related to rewards, stress, and self-control. These changes can persist well after the person has stopped using drugs. Addiction is also notably marked by periods of relapse and remission, meaning symptoms will likely return during periods of treatment noncompliance and diminish with treatment compliance. This is similar to what you see in physical conditions such as hypertension and type 2 diabetes.

Keeping all of this in mind, I will never stand by while people label those with substance use disorders as "junkies" who choose to live life crippled by their addiction. I refuse to accept that my sister, who loved her only son more than anything in the entire world, would *choose* the life she did, and the ending she did, over her son. I know for a fact that if getting sober and staying clean were easy, we would see a lot more people with addiction doing it. As close family members and loved ones of people with addiction, it's hard to see all of this while we're going through it. It's hard to love them through it. With so many disappointments and betrayals, it becomes easy to forget that it's not truly our loved ones acting out and behaving this way. It's the drugs. We tend to forget that drugs change things—major things in the brain—and the person we once loved isn't really there anymore.

One lesson became very apparent to me after this experience. Questions stemming from your loved one's addiction are not easily answered. It's almost never black and white. There's so much gray when it comes to being a family member of someone with addiction. *Do I give them money? Do I help them get into recovery? Do I cut them off completely and let them hit rock bottom? Do I let them live on the streets and pray that one day they will get their life together? Do I enable them by giving them resources they could obtain on their own? How do I support them and love them without enabling them? How do I love and support myself throughout all of this? How can I make sure I am educated and have resources? How do I face these issues and explain them to others who don't understand what I'm going through?* There are so many damn questions, and that's just the tip of the iceberg.

Being a family member of someone with opioid addiction is beyond complicated. I hope this story sheds some light on the issues we face every day as we worry about our loved ones and simply try to do our best in supporting them however we feel is right. The important takeaway is that there is no right answer for everyone. What works for one family may not work for another, just as what works for one person with opioid addiction won't work for another. It can be difficult to understand this as you're going through it or as you're seeing someone else go through it from an outsider's perspective. These are challenging issues and challenging times as we continue through a nationwide opioid crisis.

Growing up with my older sister, I never thought that I would one day be writing a book about her story to raise awareness about addiction. But here we are, and god help me, I will make Amanda's story matter. For those of you out there who are struggling just like I was, my first piece of advice would be to take care of yourself. Do whatever you need to do so that your mental health is in check. I found help in going to therapy and talking through a lot of these issues with a counselor. I also participated in Nar-Anon group meetings and got to hear stories of other family members who were going through the exact same things. This part is really important because when you realize you are not alone and there are other people out there who understand, you can find a sense of comfort and support like no other. It's not for everyone, and I understand that, but if you are struggling, I highly recommend seeking out your local Nar-Anon and Al-Anon groups. Even though my sister has passed, I still go to meetings sometimes. The sharing, trust, and understanding in those rooms is unlike anything I've ever experienced.

After Amanda died, I found myself on a spiritual journey, searching for answers and ways to connect with her now that her physical body is no longer here on Earth. In the past two years, I've learned so much related to spirituality and what happens after someone passes away. I know in my heart that my sister's soul very much lives on and that she is with me all the time. I've educated myself with books, podcasts, and other spiritual resources that have proven to me that there is more than what we see here on the physical plane. I've had several readings with psychic mediums and connected with my sister in different ways each time. The most memorable message, which will always stand out to me, came through psychic medium Natalie Miles in a reading I had in January 2020.

Natalie is one of my favorites in the spirituality world, and I've learned a lot from her podcasts and workshops. So when the opportunity came, I wasted no time scheduling a reading with her over Zoom. During the call, we talked about many things, but a large portion of our session was focused around my book and telling my sister's story. Natalie talked about how I would be "channeling her through the book" and that my sister would help me write it. She said, "Your sister will be like a co-author in this book; she has stuff to say and needs to share through this book, and it's important." She then channeled a very powerful message directly from my sister. I listened in awe as Natalie spoke.

"This was all supposed to happen this way. And that's the sole purpose of us being sisters and our lives together, so that the book could be written in this way. This is bigger than us. Don't worry about what other people think; don't worry about the family. People need to know the truth because it's not just happening in our family; it's happening in other families. So by writing this book, we are reaching other people who are experiencing the same things, so that they can find healing, power, and strength in their own beings and realize they are not alone."

For the rest of my life, I will never forget this message. And I hope I fulfilled my part of channeling her message through this book. Looking back on Amanda's life, I want to remember the good times, but I don't want to forget the bad. Those bad times were a huge part of what makes her story meaningful. As Amanda said in her message through Natalie, "This is bigger than us." And I truly believe that.

The opioid crisis goes beyond one family. Hell, it's affecting at least one family on every block throughout America. We can't ignore the problem any longer. We can't blame those struggling with addiction for their problems. Instead, we must stand together and advocate for change. We must advocate for better programming at the state level. We cannot stay silent about our stories because everyone who shares their story about addiction is helping others around them. They are helping to lift the veil, minimize the stigma around addiction, and raise awareness that this goes beyond "junkies."

Addiction has infiltrated our society as a whole. Whether it's opioids, crack, methamphetamine, or pills, our entire world has a major problem. And until we are willing to be open and talk about these things as a society, they will continue to be swept under the rug. People with addiction will continue to lie and hide in the shadows and feel the shame that society has burdened them with. It's time for change. It's time to stand together so that more people do not end up like my sister. If we can change, more people will have the opportunity, a real fighting chance, to actually *save their sister*.

With all that being said, here are six ways you can get involved or share your story to *raise awareness* about addiction and *destigmatize* these conversations in our society:

1. **Attend a support group.** Whether it be Nar-Anon, Al-Anon, or a virtual support group, there are many options to build community and have regular conversations about these issues. By participating in these meetings, you will quickly realize how similar a lot of these stories are and that you are *not alone.* These conversations may help you feel more comfortable sharing your story outside of such groups, which will ultimately help destigmatize addiction. I have started two virtual support groups that meet monthly over Zoom: Siblings of Addicts and Siblings of Addicts Who Have Passed Away. These groups are specifically for siblings, as we tend to be forgotten in a lot of family support groups related to addiction. If you would like more information on these, please reach out to me at nicole@nicolewoodruff.com. I will gladly share these resources with anyone who could use extra support.

2. **Get in touch with lawmakers.** Get involved by advocating for better programming at the state level. In Chapter 1, I shared the story of how I struggled to find my sister a quality rehab facility and quickly realized we would have to use her Medicaid insurance because private rehab was too expensive for my family to afford. Luckily, Pennsylvania has sufficient programming for state-funded drug and alcohol rehabilitation. However, not all state programming is created equal, and state programming may never compare to the quality of private-pay rehabs. All that being said, speaking up and making an impact at the state level is important. You

can download the Countable app to search upcoming and active legislation related to addiction recovery (or any issue you care about). This app also streamlines the process of contacting lawmakers to tell them how you would like them to vote on particular bills under consideration.

3. **Make a call.** Making a phone call can be one of the most effective ways to advocate. You can call the Capitol switchboard at (202) 224-3121 and locate your local member for the House and Senate. You can use the Countable app to search upcoming bills and then make calls to your local Senate and House members to advocate for their support.

4. **Volunteer.** There are many ways to do this, locally and nationwide. I recommend finding an organization you care about locally, getting involved, and donating yearly if you can. Nar-Anon or Al-Anon groups can usually point you in the right direction if you're looking for a local organization. I choose to donate to the Elizabeth Loranzo iCare Foundation, based in Middletown, Pennsylvania, because they helped Amanda pay her rent at her recovery house while she was still getting back on her feet and finding a job. This is important to me because they help provide financial resources to individuals in recovery and rely on donations to do that. For a broader list of ways you can get involved, visit https://drugfree.org/advocate-for-change/.

5. **Share your story.** Talk about your situation to your friends, neighbors, coworkers, or whomever you feel comfortable with. Every time these stories are shared, they become less taboo. People learn from your experiences, and more times than not, they will have a story to share back with you. As I've mentioned before, substance use disorders and addiction affect many families, but often we are afraid to speak up about these issues—we're embarrassed or ashamed. If we learn to treat addiction like we would treat any other physical illness, we have no reason to be ashamed. Our family member has a disease. Period. Normalize these conversations. Just as we have had a movement to normalize mental health, we need to do the same with substance use disorders.

6. **Change the way you speak about addiction.** Throughout this book, I purposely tried to avoid using the term "addict." However, when I drafted multiple early versions of this story, I didn't realize this term was problematic. I think this is important to mention. Referring to a person with substance use disorder or opioid addiction as an addict labels the person by their disease, instead of as *a human being with a disease*. Also, the word "addict" has traditionally had a negative meaning, and by defining a person solely by this term you are doing the opposite of destigmatizing addiction. Instead, use person-first language, which focuses on the person, not their illness. Try using "person with substance use disorder" or "person with opioid addiction" versus labeling

someone as an addict. Preferred terminology can be found at https://www.drugabuse.gov/drug-topics /addiction-science/words-matter-preferred-language-talking-about-addiction.

Speaking out about my family's experience with addiction is my way of giving back, even if our story doesn't have the happiest ending. I wish Amanda were still here with me to speak out about these issues, as we had originally planned before she died. I wish she had made it to the other side of addiction, to active recovery, and could speak out about her experiences and everything she learned—because many of these stories do have positive outcomes, and I think it's *incredibly important* that we share those, too. The ending of Amanda's story cannot be changed, but deep down, I know she is with me every step of the way. She is cheering me on as I spread this word and will continue to do so as we make an impact through telling her story. I will never forget the years of memories we had together. I will never forget the importance and meaning her life has brought to this world.

Amanda, I know you are with me, and I thank you for helping me find the words to write this book. I know your life wasn't easy, but I know *your story is worth it.*

In Loving Memory of Amanda Lynn Davis
April 16, 1984–June 13, 2019

ACKNOWLEDGMENTS

I started writing this book over two years ago, guided solely by intuition and trust that this message needed to be shared. I couldn't have done any of it without the love and support of my amazing husband, Cort. Thank you for your many hours of undivided attention as I wrote and edited this book. You were there for me every step of the way—listening as I read chapters aloud, giving me advice on cover design, and offering a shoulder to lean on when the weight of this became too much. I love you more than you'll ever know. Thank you for allowing this book to be possible.

To my parents and stepparents, thank you for your support and encouragement throughout this project. I know reading this isn't easy for you, but you all understand this message is more important than our feelings reading this back. And for that I'm truly grateful.

Mom, thank you for helping me throughout the writing process. Your efforts in finding important dates and helping me recall specific details of Amanda's story were invaluable.

Thank you, Aunt Anne Marie, for everything you did for Amanda towards the end of her life. You were there for her when a lot of people had given up, and I know she loved and appreciated you more than she ever fully expressed.

To Christopher, Amanda's son, whose name has been changed for privacy, thank you for allowing me to include parts of your story in order to tell your mom's. You have grown into such an amazing and incredible young man, and I'm so proud of who you have become. To Christopher's parents, thank you for all you have done and continue to do for him.

To everyone at Scribe who allowed me to bring this book to life, thank you all so much. Emily, Hussein, and Meghan, your support and coaching on our weekly calls was invaluable. To my publishing manager, Erin, thank you for your patience and always keeping me on track. To my editor, Nicole, thank you for your amazing guidance and feedback, and for helping me to bring full potential to this book. And thank you to Sheila, my cover designer, for bringing my vision to life in the cover of this book. From start to finish, the entire book writing and publishing experience with Scribe exceeded all expectations. Thank you for helping me make this idea a reality.

TIMELINE OF EVENTS

JANUARY 27, 2014—Amanda first tries heroin and shortly there after overdoses for the first time. She ends up in the emergency room and calls my mom, panicked, because her friend left her there and took off with her car. Christopher started living with us at my mom's house.

JANUARY 29 TO FEBRUARY 25, 2014—Amanda's first twenty-eight-day stay in rehab.

FEBRUARY 25, 2014—Amanda returns home from rehab and relapses the very same day. She also shares a new Facebook status: "In a Relationship."

FEBRUARY 28, 2014—Amanda overdoses for the second time, in Bloomsburg, Pennsylvania, while in the passenger seat of her car, accompanied by her new girlfriend, Shannon, who is in the driver's seat.

MARCH 1, 2014—Amanda calls to tell us she is in the Bloomsburg hospital but will not reveal what happened over the phone. Later that day, she is admitted to their psychiatric unit, where she stays for about a week.

MARCH 8, 2014—Amanda starts outpatient drug counseling.

APRIL 16, 2014—Amanda's thirtieth birthday.

APRIL 21, 2014—Amanda, Shannon, and Christopher are in a car accident on the interstate. Amanda totals her vehicle. She and Shannon are arrested following the accident for disorderly conduct after fighting alongside the highway while Christopher is with them.

APRIL 23, 2014—Amanda and Shannon show up at the house and harass Keith, our stepdad. He calls the cops, and Amanda and Shannon are charged with disorderly conduct.

APRIL 24, 2014—Amanda shows up at the house and demands money for a pack of cigarettes, screaming at the top of her lungs. We fight in my mom's kitchen until I give in and give her the money for cigarettes. I later call the cops, desperate for help.

APRIL 28, 2014—I file a 302 petition to have Amanda involuntarily hospitalized for mental health reasons, citing the fact that she is a clear and present danger to herself and others.

APRIL 28 TO MAY 9, 2014—Amanda is hospitalized in an inpatient mental health setting, where she admits to abusing Klonopin. She is diagnosed with bipolar disorder, gets her meds straightened out, and comes home a much different person.

MAY 2014—After being discharged from the inpatient psychiatric unit, Amanda starts outpatient drug counseling and medication-assisted treatment for opioid addiction.

JUNE 2014—Christopher goes back to live with Amanda and Shannon.

SEPTEMBER 18, 2014—I move to Nashville.

MARCH 2015—Child Protective Services opens a case investigating Amanda after she is reported for concerns over her drug use. My family is unaware of this at the time. The case is closed by October 2015 after Amanda complies with all requirements and remains clean. She keeps custody of Christopher and never tells my family about this case being opened.

MARCH TO DECEMBER 2015—To my family's knowledge, Amanda is still sober and doing well since being discharged from the psych hospital in May 2014. Our parents give Amanda our mom's old vehicle in March 2015 in order for her to get to work and take Christopher to appointments.

JANUARY 1, 2016—Amanda totals her new car in a single-vehicle car accident and refuses all medical treatment after the accident.

APRIL 15, 2016—Amanda overdoses on heroin laced with fentanyl while in her apartment. Christopher finds her unconscious on the kitchen floor and cannot wake her up. On the verge of dying, she is brought back with Narcan and refuses all medical attention. She is charged with reckless endangerment and endangering the welfare of a child.

APRIL 2016—Following her overdose, Amanda loses custody of Christopher. Christopher lives with my mom as he finishes out the rest of the school year.

MAY 31, 2016—Temporary custody is granted to Christopher's father, but Christopher alternates between staying with my mom and his dad for the summer of 2016.

JULY 29 TO AUGUST 26, 2016—Amanda goes to rehab for the second time.

END OF AUGUST 2016—Christopher moves in with his dad full time and starts the new school year where his dad lives, about two hours away from my family.

EARLY SEPTEMBER 2016—Amanda relapses shortly after being discharged from rehab.

WINTER 2016—Amanda sentenced to two years' probation under the ARD program.

EARLY 2017—Amanda starts using again but continues to deny this to my family. She barely keeps in touch with me, so I'm confident she has relapsed.

JULY 4, 2017—I receive alarming videos from my mom of Amanda high on heroin. This is the worst any of us has ever seen her. In the videos, she continues to deny she is on any drugs. Later that evening, I reach out to my friend Ian, who is a former probation officer, and ask him for help in getting in touch with the county's probation office.

JULY 6 OR 7, 2017—Ian gets back in touch and tells me Amanda will have to report to probation soon; we just have to give it a few days.

JULY 10, 2017—Amanda is contacted by probation and needs to report. She starts asking who reported her and is very angry with my family.

JULY TO OCTOBER 2017—Amanda is followed more closely by a probation officer and is given random drug screenings. However, she fails drug test after drug test for months and falls further into her heroin and methamphetamine addiction. During this time, Amanda loses more than fifty pounds.

OCTOBER 26 TO NOVEMBER 22, 2017—Amanda finally agrees to go back to inpatient drug rehab. This is her third time in as many years.

NOVEMBER 22, 2017, TO FEBRUARY 2018—Amanda enters a recovery house for the first time. She starts outpatient drug counseling, attends NA meetings, and receives medication-assisted treatment, particularly the Vivitrol shot.

MID- TO LATE FEBRUARY 2018—Amanda is kicked out of her recovery house. I help Amanda rent a room at a new house (not a recovery house) nearby.

LATE FEBRUARY/EARLY MARCH 2018—Amanda relapses on bath salts with Shannon.

MID- TO LATE MARCH 2018—Amanda gets kicked out of the new house where she has been renting a room. She convinces my mom to put her up in a hotel for three days, where she and Shannon do nothing but use heroin the entire time.

THREE DAYS LATER, MARCH 2018—Amanda calls everyone in my family, asking for more money to continue staying at the hotel. I warn everyone that she is using, and we all cut her off financially. We offer to pick Amanda up and take her back to rehab, but she chooses to stay with Shannon on the streets instead.

ONE DAY LATER, MARCH 2018—Amanda calls me and says she will go back to rehab.

MARCH 28 TO APRIL 23, 2018—Amanda is admitted to her fourth inpatient drug rehab in as many years.

APRIL 23, 2018—Amanda transitions to a new recovery house in Lemoyne, Pennsylvania.

SEPTEMBER 29, 2018—Amanda attends my wedding in Nashville, Tennessee.

MARCH 28 TO DECEMBER 2018—Amanda has her longest stretch of sobriety.

MID-DECEMBER 2018—Amanda is kicked out of her recovery house in Lemoyne due to taking too much of one of her prescriptions. I help Amanda temporarily rent a room at a house in downtown Harrisburg, Pennsylvania.

WEEK AFTER CHRISTMAS 2018—Amanda has a supervised weekend with Christopher at my mom's house. According to my mom, Amanda sleeps a lot and seems out of it. My mom and Amanda argue throughout the weekend.

JANUARY 24, 2019—Amanda admits to me that she relapsed after I try a new approach to confront her.

JANUARY 25, 2019—My mom and Keith pick Amanda up in Harrisburg and bring her back to their house to stay for a few days until she can get her Vivitrol shot and get back into a recovery house.

JANUARY 28, 2019—Amanda gets her Vivitrol shot and enters a new recovery house in Harrisburg.

END OF JANUARY TO MID-MARCH 2019—Amanda does well, communicates with me often, and attends NA meetings. She appears committed to her recovery.

MID-MARCH 2019—Amanda starts acting differently; relapse warning signs are present.

MAY 2019—Amanda has extensive dental work (full teeth extractions) and struggles afterwards with pain, adjusting to dentures, and her appearance.

END OF MAY 2019—It starts to become clear to me that Amanda isn't doing well. She answers my texts less frequently and rarely reaches out to me.

MAY 27, 2019—I message Amanda with a similar approach to what I used after her last relapse in January 2018. She admits she used a "couple of times" and was kicked out of her recovery house. Says she is staying with a guy she met online. We come up with a similar plan to her last relapse, and she says she will schedule her Vivitrol shot ASAP.

MAY 28, 2019—Amanda tells me she needs to be out of the guy's house by Friday, May 31. She says her Vivitrol shot is scheduled for Tuesday, June 4.

MAY 31, 2019—Although Amanda originally said she needed to be out of the guy's house on this date, she Ubers back there after work and ends up staying another night.

JUNE 1, 2019—At 1:00 p.m., Amanda messages me and says she needs to be out of the guy's house by 6:00 p.m. She says she is "freaking out" because she has nowhere to go. She also says she can stay with another guy in Carlisle, but doesn't want to. We argue, but she gives me no other choice than to put her up in a hotel for a few days. I pay for Amanda to stay three nights in a Howard Johnson hotel located near the Dollar General where she works in Harrisburg.

JUNE 2, 2019—Amanda tells me she thinks she found a recovery house and will reach out to the woman in charge. She sends me information about the place.

JUNE 4, 2019—Amanda supposedly gets her Vivitrol shot.

JUNE 5, 2019—Amanda tells me she has pink eye and needs to go to urgent care. For the rest of the day, I do not hear from her. She is supposed to be out of the hotel by now, but she continues to stay there and pay for it somehow. In the meantime, I fly to Nashville to attend CMA Fest and prepare to move out of my Nashville home.

JUNE 6, 2019—Amanda tells me she is going to stay at the hotel another night because "no one's is going to let me go anywhere today with pink eye." I ask Amanda if she has been getting high, and she tells me no. I don't hear from her for the rest of the night.

JUNE 7, 2019—I don't hear from Amanda again that morning, and she doesn't answer several of my text messages. I break down and call her several times before she answers. Amanda finally admits she is using and did *not* get her Vivitrol shot on Tuesday, despite me giving her gas money to go see her addiction doctor to get the shot. This is the last time I speak to her over the phone.

JUNE 8, 2019—Amanda texts me "I am safe & I love you. I want to have a long talk with you tomorrow." This is the last time I ever hear from her.

JUNE 9 AND 10, 2019—No word from Amanda. I prepare to pack up and move out of my Nashville home.

JUNE 11, 2019—I call the Howard Johnson hotel to check to see if Amanda is still there. They tell me she checked out.

JUNE 12, 2019—My mom receives a message from Shannon telling her that she is worried about Amanda because she hasn't heard from her in several days and can't get a hold of her. I file a missing person's report with the local police in Harrisburg. A police officer also stops by the Howard Johnson hotel to see if Amanda is there. They tell him she has checked out.

JUNE 13, 2019—Hotel staff find Amanda dead in her hotel room. She has overdosed on IV fentanyl. I later receive a call from the Dauphin County coroner.

JUNE 22, 2019—Amanda's memorial service is held in our home town, Minersville, Pennsylvania.

www.ingramcontent.com/pod-product-compliance
Lightning Source LLC
Chambersburg PA
CBHW021844090426
42811CB00033B/2128/J